MW01224247

take a closer look

take a closer look

*Uncommon and Unexpected Insights
That Will Change Your Life*

Bryan McAnally

HOWARD BOOKS

A DIVISION OF SIMON & SCHUSTER

New York   London   Toronto   Sydney

Our purpose at Howard Books is to:
· *Increase faith* in the hearts of growing Christians
· *Inspire holiness* in the lives of believers
· *Instill hope* in the hearts of struggling people everywhere
Because He's coming again!

Published by Howard Books, a division of Simon & Schuster, Inc.
1230 Avenue of the Americas, New York, NY 10020
www.howardpublishing.com

Take a Closer Look © 2007 by GRQ, Inc.

All rights reserved, including the right to reproduce this book or portions thereof in any form whatsoever. For information, address Howard Subsidiary Rights Department, Simon & Schuster, 1230 Avenue of the Americas, New York, NY 10020.

ISBN 13: 978-1-4165-4213-1
ISBN 10:   1-4165-4213-2
ISBN 13: 978-1-58229-686-9 (gift edition)
ISBN 10:   1-58229-686-3 (gift edition)

10 9 8 7 6 5 4 3 2 1

HOWARD and colophon are registered trademarks of Simon & Schuster, Inc.
Manufactured in the United States of America

For information regarding special discounts for bulk purchases, please contact: Simon & Schuster Special Sales at 1-800-456-6798 or business@simonandschuster.com.

Managing Editor: Lila Empson
Associate Editor: Chrys Howard
Design: Whisner Design Group

Scripture quotations noted cev are from the *Contemporary English Version*. Copyright © 1995 by American Bible Society. Used by permission. Scripture quotations noted esv are from *The Holy Bible, English Standard Version*, copyright © 2001 by Crossway Bibles, a division of Good News Publishers. Used by Permission. All rights reserved. Scripture quotations noted hcsb have been taken from the *Holman Christian Standard Bible®*; Copyright © 1999, 2000, 2002, 2003 by Holman Bible Publishers. Used by permission. *Holman Christian Standard Bible®*, Holman CSB® and HCSB® are federally registered trademarks of Holman Bible Publishers. Scripture quotations noted msg are from *The Message*. Copyright © by Eugene H. Peterson 1993, 1994, 1995. Used by permission of NavPress Publishing Group. Scripture quotations noted nasb are from the *New American Standard Bible®*, copyright © 1960, 1962, 1963, 1968, 1971, 1973, 1975, 1977, 1995 by The Lockman Foundation. Used by permission. Scripture quotations noted ncv are from *The Holy Bible, New Century Version*, copyright © 1987, 1988, 1991 by Word Publishing, a division of Thomas Nelson, Inc. All rights reserved. Used by permission. Scripture quotations noted niv are from the *Holy Bible: New International Version®*. Copyright © 1973, 1978, 1984 by International Bible Society. Used by permission of Zondervan Publishing House. All rights reserved. Scripture quotations noted nkjv are from *The New King James Version®*. Copyright © 1979, 1980, 1982 by Thomas Nelson, Inc. Used by permission. All rights reserved. Scripture quotations noted nlt are from the *Holy Bible, New Living Translation*, copyright © 1996. Used by permission of Tyndale House Publishers, Inc., Wheaton, Illinois 60189. All rights reserved.

You reveal the path of life to me;
in Your presence is abundant joy;
in Your right hand are eternal pleasures.

Psalm 16:11 HCSB

Contents

Introduction

The Bible is the most provocative book ever published. It contains the most revolutionary words and the most compelling message imaginable. This text has been translated into more than a thousand languages, with more translations being undertaken every year. This text has been the source of international conflict, social uprising, and cultural revolution. At the same time, it has brought peace, imparted hope, and transformed the lives of the millions of people who read it. It has divided individual families, only to later unite them as its members came to understand its singular message.

A young child can embrace the Bible's basic message yet spend the rest of his life learning and applying its implications. The Bible's chapters contain history, prose, poetry, typology, allusion, counsel, song, and prophecy. Its text is to be viewed and reviewed; it offers new insight, sudden relevance, and contemporary perspective each time it passes before human eyes.

For all it offers, the Bible requires only that it be read to unlock its potential. The Bible refers to itself as "the Word," using two different Greek terms as an explanation. The first, *logos*, speaks to that which the Bible shares with every other printed text. It is simply a message that is communicated for all who will receive it. However, the same word elsewhere is translated from the Greek *rhema*, which speaks to the personal power available when the Bible's text is applied to a person's life. In this regard, a closed Bible offers little special value; it must be opened and read before its power can be accessed.

Even if you have grown up reading its pages, memorizing its stories, or considering its claims, take a closer look at the familiar passages in the pages that follow. Discover a new, power-packed, and personal perspective. Experience a fresh encounter with the most inviting book in history, and embrace the adventure in store especially for you.

God means what he says. What he says goes. His powerful Word is sharp as a surgeon's scalpel, cutting through everything, whether doubt or defense, laying us open to listen and obey. Nothing and no one is impervious to God's Word. We can't get away from it—no matter what.

Hebrews 4:12–13 MSG

C. S. Lewis

*God cannot give us a happiness
and peace apart from Himself,
because it is not there. There
is no such thing.*

You wisely and tenderly lead me,
and then you bless me.

Psalm 73:24 MSG

Let's Begin

In the beginning God created the heavens and the earth.

Genesis 1:1 HCSB

The Big Picture

Close your eyes and think of nothing. It is virtually impossible to capture "nothing." Within moments, your senses will give in, overloaded and overcome by a cavalcade of sounds, smells, flavors, sensations, and experiences that abound all around. Do you hear that bird outside, or the hum of an appliance? Do you smell the spices from your last meal, or of a candle that burns? Are thoughts of a project at work sneaking in, or are you surprised to be suddenly making a list of what you need at the store?

It is so hard to comprehend that there was a time when there was nothing. The Bible begins with an introduction to that time. Genesis 1 welcomes you to the time when there was nothing . . . except God.

The words "In the beginning God" announce that before there was anything, God existed. At "the beginning," God was there. And it was God who—within the Bible's first ten words—caused creation to explode everywhere in an obedient response to the voice of God. From nothing, God commanded that the heavens and the earth exist.

take a CLOSER look

And it was so.

Bara, the Hebrew word for "created," is used elsewhere in the Old Testament to show that God's creative actions are unique and unprecedented. Nowhere is this more evident than in this example of the spoken word of the Creator; out of nothing sprang forth something. The heavens were born above and around the formless and dark earth. Again, God spoke and light immediately burst forth universally, separating from the dark. Then, in the parade of creation, out marched the waters of the seas, green plants to cover the lands, and animals of every stripe and breed. At the height of it all, God made humans, a man and a woman.

At each stage of creation, God assessed the work he had accomplished by the power of his will. He evaluated what he had made and established it as "good." God effectively and efficiently created a home for all people of all time, which, by his own assessment, was excellent for every need and purpose. The man and the woman could and would use everything that God had provided for them. God had made everything for them and all who would come from them.

What a time it must have been.

We know that God causes all things to work together for good to those who love God, to those who are called according to His purpose.

Romans 8:28 NASB

Take a Closer Look

Take a closer look at the phrase "In the beginning" and see that before God created anything else, he created time. With these first words of Scripture, God not only started working, he also started the clock framing your life's existence.

God has no need for time; he operates completely outside of it. He exists independently of it. The fact that he chose to create time shows that God has a plan. His plan has a beginning and an ending. "In the beginning" was the initiation of that plan. Everything that has happened since was also perfectly planned. When God evaluated each phase of creation as "good," he did so knowing the full history of it.

Time is the tool God devised to complete his plan. Everything he created has a place and a purpose in that plan. Light does not just make the world easier to see; it marks daily progress toward the culmination of the Master Plan. Rain is not a coincidental natural event; it is a necessary, important part of God's good plan. Because everything that exists does so within time toward the completion of God's plan, everything is under control.

> Time is God's way of keeping everything from happening at once.
>
> Author Unknown

time = plan

Do not overlook the amazing reality that God has remembered you in his plan. If the creation of time—the capsule within which every other creation follows—shows that God has a plan, the fact that you live daily within the universal drama of time shows that you are included in his dynamic plan. His "in the beginning" was the initiation of that plan, and there will one day be a completion to it. This is true for the universe, and it is true for you.

Apply It
to Your Life

You have been part of God's eternal plan, accounted for before time. God remembered you and prepared creation for you—the air you would breathe, the food you would eat, the friends you would find, and even the rainbow you would see. And don't forget that God keeps his promises.

In a world that says you are a product of cosmic coincidence and that life has no meaning, God says otherwise. He is telling you that he is in control. You can trust him. With Genesis 1, he wants you to know that before the beginning of time, God thought of you. In the busy pace of a hectic life, God is here, and he has made time for you.

We know that there is only one God, the Father, who created everything, and we exist for him. And there is only one Lord, Jesus Christ, through whom God made everything and through whom we have been given life.

1 Corinthians 8:6 NLT

Scientific theories have futilely attempted to account for the universe's supernatural beginning with a natural explanation. To this, pastor and theologian Dr. John MacArthur said:

"Genesis 1:1 gives a general and inclusive account of creation. . . . He [God] is the creator of all things visible and invisible, and 'all things' means everything from various ranks of angels, every form of life from whales and elephants to viruses. Everything, all things include every form of energy, every form of matter, the speed of light, nuclear structure, electromagnetism, gravity, every law by which nature operates was created within the framework of this creation."

Saint Augustine of Hippo, in his classic *City of God*, explains that this reality confounds many:

"It is no wonder that those theorists wander in a circuitous maze finding neither entrance nor exit for they do not know how the human race, and this mortal condition of ours, first started nor with what end it will be brought to a close. They cannot penetrate the 'depth of God,' the deep counsel of which, being himself eternal and without beginning, he started man and time from a beginning, and made man in time, as a new act of creation, and yet with no sudden change in purpose, but in accordance with his eternal and unchanging plan."

Zooming **In**

Exodus 20:11 declares that God created in six days. On the seventh day, he rested. In this, humanity has both a straightforward explanation of how the world came to be and also a clear principle that even the most diligent, dedicated workers need to take time to rest from the hard work that fills the rest of life.

Genesis 1:1 offers the first reference to God in the Bible—the Hebrew word for "God" is *elohim*—a plural noun. This serves to introduce the Christian teaching of the Trinity, that God is three-in-one. This doctrine that God the Father, God the Son, and God the Holy Spirit are one, coequal and coeternal, is consistently presented throughout both the Old and New Testaments.

God - one but with plural names

Yesterday was no coincidence. Today is no accident. Tomorrow has a plan. God made time and placed you in it with everything you would ever need, so you would know him and his purpose.

Through the
Eyes of
Your Heart

If time is God's tool, then the many places in the Bible that read, "it came to pass," show that God is at work in the lives of people. Have you ever felt as though a bad time would never end? Think of how God worked to move you through that situation.

*prayer - it came
signs of hope*

Think of an important lesson you learned earlier in life. What were the circumstances that taught you that lesson? How is an unpleasant time made more bearable through these learned lessons?

be kind / compassionate

Time often provides a new perspective. When have you gone through a tough time only to be thankful later? How did the passage of time change your mind?

*priorities change
clarity in situations
* Truth*

All's Well That Ends Well

When Isaac's servants dug in the valley and found there a well of flowing water, the herdsmen of Gerar quarreled with the herdsmen of Isaac. . . . Then they dug another well, and they quarreled over it too. . . . He moved away from there and dug another well, and they did not quarrel over it; so he named it Rehoboth, for he said, "At last the LORD has made room for us, and we will be fruitful in the land."

Genesis 26:19–22 NASB

The
Big Picture

Isaac, the son of Abraham, had just buried his father. As Abraham's sole heir and favored son, Isaac also assumed complete responsibility over the entire family, as well as over the family's successful farming and ranching business. Soon after, a drought swept Israel, and Isaac knew he must relocate to survive. At God's leading, Isaac settled his family in Gerar, the land of his enemies, the Philistines. He experienced immediate success, his holdings increased dramatically, and his family prospered.

While Isaac's wealth and prominence expanded over the years he spent in Gerar, his popularity did not. As he became increasingly powerful, the Philistines' envy drove them to convince their king to give him a royal eviction. Isaac and his family packed their belongings and moved to a nearby valley. Again, he immediately went to work uncovering the abandoned wells of his youth, which the Philistines had buried in an attempt to erase Isaac's right of ownership. Those wells had long ago either run dry or become stag-

take a CLOSER look

nant. He met no opposition as he rebuilt and renamed the wells, using the same names given by his father.

When Isaac excavated a well for his livestock, he was not digging simply for water. He undertook this arduous task to claim ownership upon the acreage surrounding the well. The wells were not just sources of provision; they were also monumental statements of property.

Problems for Isaac sprang forth when his enterprising herdsmen expanded their master's territory by digging new wells for his flocks. When the Philistine herdsmen of Gerar heard news that Isaac's men had unearthed a spring well flowing with water, they immediately contended for the ownership rights. Rather than fight, Isaac relented and let the Philistines benefit from his and his men's labor. Unbelievably, it took Isaac's men two more tries before they dug a well that the Philistines did not contest. He at last had a new well, and new land where his family could prosper.

More remarkable than Isaac's perseverance is the fact that Isaac did not set up camp at this well he had named Rehoboth, where he praised God for a peaceful location. Almost immediately, Isaac led his tribe back to Beersheba, where his father had first heard the promise of God. There, he dug yet another well, and this time, Isaac pitched his tent. Four wells and two disagreements later, Isaac had settled in the land God had provided.

There are four steps to accomplishment:
Plan purposefully. Prepare prayerfully.
Proceed positively. Pursue persistently.

Author Unknown

Take a closer look at Isaac's controversial well digging and see the subtle lesson of how patience led him to persevere peacefully through his difficulties.

Isaac needed resources to keep things growing for his expanding herds. Twice denying Isaac the right to dig these vital wells, the Philistines jealously contended his rights because they did not want him as a foreigner to succeed while they toiled.

Isaac could have obtained by force what he was claiming by rights. Yet both times Isaac declined to press the issue. He understood what it meant to pick his battles. He recognized that in God's vast land, there was more than enough room for him and his family. He understood that God used these conflicts to reveal that better solutions lay elsewhere. Isaac's proper perspective showed that the only way to win in the long run was by giving up these wells. Keeping the controversial wells meant forsaking the land God had promised.

Perseverance during troublesome times allowed Isaac to understand where to look for God's blessing. Focusing on God's promises enabled Isaac to recognize God's provision when it finally arrived. Isaac understood that Rehoboth's peace was actually a sign of God's blessing.

> *God is worth waiting for. We ought not to prejudge the great drama of life, but stay till the closing scene, and see to what a finis the whole arrives.*
>
> Charles Spurgeon

You, too, will face conflict. Isaac's example demonstrates that arguments can be both an obstacle denying God's blessing as well as a signpost directing you toward it, depending upon your response.

Isaac faced a decision that is common in today's world. The Philistines hassled him because they wanted to keep success for themselves. He had to decide whether he was going to fight and take by force what was rightfully his or seek a less confrontational, more peaceful solution. Isaac gave up his rights twice when he realized that winning a war over contested wells would cost him much more in the end.

In this competitive world, almost any confrontation can be a conflict-in-waiting. Isaac showed that it was better to surrender a small fight to win the more important battle. In his case—and in most cases—people can get so focused on winning the most immediate conflict that they end up losing focus of the larger objective.

You should always decide if the battle you win today comes at a cost you would rather not pay. Instead, seek peace by persevering through ugly situations. Not only will you avoid unnecessary conflict, but you will see the great ways God always keeps his promises.

Blessed are the meek, for they will inherit the earth. . . .
Blessed are the peacemakers, for they will be called
sons of God.

Matthew 5:5, 9 NIV

Patience is a bittersweet blessing; it is manifested only when facing difficult circumstances requiring it. Matthew Henry, in *Matthew Henry's Commentary: Genesis to Deuteronomy*, said:

"Those that open the fountains of truth must expect contradiction. . . . What is often the lot even of the most quiet and peaceable men in this world; those that avoid striving yet cannot being striven with. . . . What a mercy it is to have plenty of water, to have it without striving for it. . . . Those that follow peace, sooner or later, shall find peace; those that study to be quiet seldom fail of being so."

And Adam Clarke, in *Adam Clarke's Commentary: Genesis 26*, said:

"Never did any man more implicitly follow the Divine command, Resist not evil, than Isaac; whenever he found that his work was likely to be a subject of strife and contention, he gave place, and rather chose to suffer wrong than to have his own peace of mind disturbed. Thus he overcame evil with good."

Zooming **In**

Isaac took time to name the first wells he ultimately relinquished to the Philistines. He named the wells *Esek* and *Sitnah*, which in Hebrew mean "contention" and "opposition," respectively. With these names, Isaac forever commemorated the strife associated with these wellsprings, leaving the Philistines a reminder that they had to consider every time they drew water from them.

The flourishing city of Gerar was located between Gaza and Beersheba, on the edge of Canaanite territory. It was home to the Philistines, pagans who made treaties with both Abraham and Isaac but who would later wage war against Israel during the age of Israel's kings. The Philistines were well established historically and were mentioned in documents of Egyptian and Assyrian historians.

In the heat of the moment, keeping your mouth closed and not fighting back are rarely the first natural responses. Yet if you choose these supernatural options, you will show more might through meekness than you ever will by striking back.

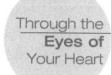

Through the
Eyes of
Your Heart

It is only human to want to defend yourself, but that is not always the best choice. Is your first response to fight back or to find a peaceful solution? Would you consider the peaceful option if you thought it held more hope for long-term success? *be quiet — retreat or peaceful — Fair Win/win solution*

Seeking peace is risky because you have to be vulnerable. What scares you most about appearing vulnerable to those who want to take advantage of you? *that I am weak / a pushover*

To find the peaceable solution, not only do you have to be vulnerable, but also optimistic. What benefits do you see by chasing peace? *longer lasting, better energy, more happiness with collaboration*

A Question of Healing

Crowds of sick people—blind, lame, or paralyzed—lay on the porches. One of the men lying there had been sick for thirty-eight years. When Jesus saw him and knew how long he had been ill, he asked him, "Would you like to get well?" "I can't, sir," the sick man said, "for I have no one to help me into the pool when the water is stirred up. While I am trying to get there, someone else always gets in ahead of me." Jesus told him, "Stand up, pick up your sleeping mat, and walk!" Instantly, the man was healed! He rolled up the mat and began walking!

John 5:3–9 NLT

The Big Picture

Jesus began his brief ministry on earth by immediately sharing the good news of God's love. To show this love, Jesus performed many miracles. He cured sickness, disease, and defects. He offered hope and forgiveness to many hurting people. His reputation grew widely and rapidly. Crowds flocked to Jesus and followed him as he traveled. In John 5, Jesus approached Jerusalem to take part in a religious feast. He traveled south from Galilee, where the Bible says only a few days earlier he had spent time with the Samaritan people and paused to heal a nobleman's son known to be dying from a terminal illness. As Jesus approached Jerusalem to enter the city where the religious ceremonies would be held, he had to navigate through the crowds of people gathered at Bethesda, a network of five natural springs forming pools on the outskirts of town outside Jerusalem's gate.

As Jesus walked among the people amassed there, it was apparent why these people lingering at Bethesda's edge would not have come to Jesus for healing. The people lying poolside were not important, beautiful, popular, or powerful. They were not vacationing, sunbathing, or taking a leisurely retreat. Bethesda was no spa. Bethesda's patrons were infirm and crippled. These were crowds of some of the most unhealthy, unpleasant, unattractive people in the land. They had been cut off from society and relegated to the springs outside the city walls, accessible through a gate most commonly used to herd sacrificial sheep in and out of Jerusalem. They had gathered there because the pools were known for healing waters believed to cure sicknesses, diseases, and deformities that had plagued and isolated the people from their friends, families, and community. Whenever the pools stirred, the people would rush to the waters with hopes for healing.

It was there that Jesus met the unnamed man in focus. This sad man had lain away from the water for thirty-eight long years due to paralysis. He had no friends. His family was nowhere to be found. He did not even have the dignity of his own mobility. However, through a brief discussion in which Jesus spoke a simple command, God accomplished more in a moment than had the man's nearly forty years of superstition and frustration.

Take the first step in faith. You do not have to see the whole staircase, just take the first step.

Martin Luther King Jr.

Take a
Closer Look

A closer look at this miracle reveals that Jesus was more concerned about the paralyzed man's faith than he was about his ability to walk. Jesus asked the man, "Do you want to get better?"

What an unusual question! He did not ask how the man had become paralyzed or how long he had been stranded on the water's edge. Jesus went straight to the heart of the matter and asked if the man truly desired to be made well.

The paralytic gave perhaps the most disappointing answer possible. First, he blamed his paralysis. From there, he blamed others—nobody would carry him down in time for healing. Finally, he blamed God by sharing an incorrect belief in the legend that God worked through an angel that stirred the waters. This man was in a desperate condition—not only could he not walk, but he had no faith!

None of this surprised Jesus. He knew that no parable would comfort this man's sorrow. No spiritual encouragement would erase this man's despair. Instead, Jesus gave the man nothing less than a miracle. He gave the man a command to rise and walk.

> In almost every case the beginning of new blessing is a new revelation of the character of God—more beautiful, more wonderful, more precious.
>
> J. Elder Cumming

God still asks people if they truly want to be made well. Every day, debilitated people give wrong answers to the right question. Maybe they have physical limitations or disfigurements. Maybe they have been victimized and have lost all hope. Maybe they have mistakenly bought in to misleading traditions, myths, legends, or fables.

Maybe they think God is simply out of blessings and they have missed their chance at a new life. Yet Jesus still asks because he is eager to meet the needs of those who will take a step of faith.

There may be something in your life that has left you spiritually paralyzed, physically hindered, or emotionally injured. Living in debilitation is safe because it is predictable; but it is also restricting, isolating, and frustrating. God offers you today the same opportunity that he offered the paralytic back then. Your inability to carry on independently is far less important than your ability to believe in the power of God. Set aside excuses and flex your faith muscles. When that happens, miracles inevitably follow. The first blessing is belief. Everything after that will be as natural as putting one foot in front of the other.

If anyone is in Christ, there is a new creation; old things have passed away, and look, new things have come.

2 Corinthians 5:17 HCSB

In meeting the paralytic at the well, Jesus showed how God will go to the farthest length to meet needs and bring hope. John Emmons said:

"The African impala can jump to a height of over 10 feet and cover a distance of greater than 30 feet. Yet these magnificent creatures can be kept in an enclosure in any zoo with a 3-foot wall. The animals will not jump if they cannot see where their feet will fall. Faith is the ability to trust what we cannot see, and with faith we are freed from the flimsy enclosures of life that only fear allows to entrap us."

E. Stanley Jones said:

"I am inwardly fashioned for faith, not for fear. Fear is not my native land; faith is. I am so made that worry and anxiety are sand in the machinery of life; faith is the oil. I live better by faith and confidence than by fear, doubt and anxiety. In anxiety and worry, my being is gasping for breath—these are not my native air. But in faith and confidence, I breathe freely—these are my native air."

Zooming **In**

In Jesus' day, disabilities were thought to be the punishing consequence of sin. The paralytic was considered unclean and unapproachable. No righteous religious person would go near him. God's forgiveness seemed impossible. In healing a man perceived stricken due to sin, Jesus performed a miracle considered scandalous. His cure implied that Jesus forgave sins, a feat reserved for God alone.

In 1888, while the Church of Saint Anne underwent repairs, archaeologists working near Nehemiah's "sheep gate" uncovered a reservoir that had once filled two pools. There they discovered a fresco of an angel stirring the pools' waters. Bethesda had been found! The word *Bethesda* is a Greek transliteration of a Hebrew word meaning "house of outpouring."

Faith often requires action that seems impossible apart from God. Trust Jesus to meet your most basic spiritual needs; this first step is the starting point in your spiritual journey.

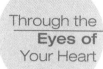

Through the
Eyes of
Your Heart

You can trust God today because his fingerprints can be found all through your life, bringing you to this moment of belief. Where else in your life has God picked you up and given you faith?

Personal events seem to happen for a reason. How have experiences brought you to where you are today?

Sometimes people inadvertently get in their own way. What hindering excuses or obstacles do you have to set aside to receive God's blessings today?

The Weight of Suffering

As they led him away, they seized Simon from Cyrene, who was on his way in from the country, and put the cross on him and made him carry it behind Jesus.

Luke 23:26 NIV

The Big Picture

The streets of Jerusalem were filled with worshippers arriving from around the region to celebrate Passover. It was common for Jewish people to make Passover pilgrimages to Jerusalem. For many, the journey to Jerusalem was itself an act of worship as they obeyed God's command to remember his liberation of the people of Israel from Egyptian slavery. That foreign believers traveled so far marked the depth of their faith and fidelity.

One such worshiper was Simon, who the Bible reports was a citizen of Cyrene. Simon came from a city on Libya's northeast seaboard. For Simon even to be a part of Jerusalem's celebration was significant; he journeyed more than nine hundred miles to be there. Simon was a serious follower of God.

Passover worshipers came focused upon God. Many of these same folks clogging Jerusalem's byways had only days earlier noisily hailed Jesus as the one coming in the name of the Lord. They covered the dusty streets with leafy branches and even with their clothes to make his pathway clean and straight! They had made such a buzz that locals stopped to ask who Jesus was and why he was so important.

It is not known if Simon had been part of the crowd that had earlier worshiped Jesus, but it is easy to imagine Simon's surprise when he unexpectedly found himself face-to-face with a contingent of Roman soldiers and an angry mob, all marching Jesus to his death while forcing him to drag his own cross.

For some reason, these Roman soldiers chose Simon from the crowd and forced the foreigner to carry Jesus' cross. They did not ask, and he had not offered. As a Jewish believer, he was one for whom the Romans had low regard and high disdain. To the mocking soldiers who had just beaten and abused Jesus, Simon was nothing more than an unwilling participant in their cruel game. Simon was forced not only to bear the weight of the cross, but he was also forced to share the suffering of Jesus.

Character cannot be developed in ease and quiet. Only through experience of trial and suffering can the soul be strengthened, vision cleared, ambition inspired, and success achieved.

Helen Keller

The Bible does not tell much about Simon, but a closer look at his story shows the surprising nature of suffering. Simon did not get to pick the moment of his inconvenience. Simon's actions show that even when misfortune is thrust upon you, your response can be a courageous act of faith that demonstrates God's care over your life.

Simon was not merely inconvenienced by being forced to carry Jesus' cross. It was a tool designed for killing. Men carrying the cross marched toward the hill of Golgotha, where they would be strapped to the cross to die a horribly painful death. If they fell along the way, they would be whipped and battered. Meanwhile, crowds of mockers would torment them. Simon wanted no part in Jesus' agony. Any person would certainly have to be forced to endure such subjection and torture.

When everybody was marching to crucify Jesus, Simon was simply a man passing by "on his way in from the country." He was not looking for trouble; he simply wanted to join the religious ceremonies of the day. None of this mattered, as he was forced to change direction and share the agony of Jesus.

> *The cross is easier for him who takes it up than for him who drags it behind.*
>
> Author Unknown

Have you ever felt like Simon the Cyrene? Just going through life, trying to be a good person who wants to please God and not make trouble, then suddenly you are smack-dab in the middle of a calamity. Criticism, accusations, or inconvenience—you find yourself being persecuted, and you cannot even think of a reason to explain why it is happening.

Apply It
to Your Life

In times like that, the pain may be great, and you may feel completely alone. Yet God brings good news even in the middle of your suffering.

Simon was quickly forgotten by the angry soldiers who turned their attention to crucifying Jesus. Your difficult times, too, will pass. In the relay of suffering, you have been handed Simon's baton, but you do not run the anchor in this race. The suffering you face is ultimately not your own, and Christ has already taken the ultimate burden upon the cross. You are a partner in Jesus' suffering, partaking in his cross for a time and distance in life. Subsequently, burdens are only temporary. Like Simon, you will be released from suffering's weight. Keep moving forward by faith. God will sustain you.

*He said to them all, "If anyone desires to come after Me,
let him deny himself, and take up his cross daily,
and follow Me."*

Luke 9:23 NKJV

Suffering, as demonstrated by Simon the Cyrene, has a purpose in life. While never pleasant at the time, these experiences can bring a cherished perspective. Bob Deffinbaugh said:

"There is a distinct emphasis here . . . the Holy Spirit was conveying through Luke's words. Luke has been constructing this text in a way that would highlight the contrast between the cruelty of men and the compassion of the Lord Jesus, Who thinks not of His own suffering, but of those who follow after Him, mourning. It is unbelieving men who are cruel, and it is God Who is kind, contrary to many popular misconceptions of God and man."

Rod Keesee said:

"Of course, the deed he performed was to help Jesus carry the stake on which He would soon suffer crucifixion. While it may seem a little difficult to put ourselves in Simon's place, it is important to think about what he actually did. In a very critical time and circumstance, Simon gave of himself to the Savior of all mankind."

Zooming In

The cross was a method of death created by Romans and used exclusively on non-Romans. The torturous tool was so feared and reviled that, according to the Roman author Cicero, people were afraid to utter the word *cross* and were encouraged to not look upon one, much less even think about someone's dying by way of one.

Mark's Gospel is commonly considered the apostle Peter's account penned by Mark, written to early followers of Jesus. This message mentions Simon of Cyrene's sons Alexander and Rufus by name, giving insight that Simon's suffering resulted in the blessing of his boys' eventually becoming Christians themselves. They witnessed his example and chose to follow Jesus as well.

In the bottom of suffering's valley, it is difficult to see the big picture with a heavenly perspective. Remember that God's will for you is good, and hard times are not here to stay.

Suffering is difficult to handle, especially if it comes unexpectedly. How have you been surprised by suffering in the past? What surprised you about it? How did you react to the situation?

s ha

sudden

God can use any circumstance for his will, even if the situation seems unexplainable at the time. Simon suffered, but history shows he was in the right place at the right time. What good has come out of your past times of suffering?

shared suffering

It is a privilege to feel and to know God's presence in your life. Simon was able to watch Jesus' every step on the way to Golgotha. Where do you sense Christ supporting you, sustaining you in your difficulties?

Between a Rock and a Hard Place

> *Moses said to the people, "Do not be afraid. Stand still, and see the salvation of the LORD, which He will accomplish for you today. For the Egyptians whom you see today, you shall see again no more forever. The LORD will fight for you, and you shall hold your peace."*
>
> Exodus 14:13–14 NKJV

The Big Picture

Camping in the plain of Pi Hahiroth, the Jewish nation heard a rumbling thunder. Yet no storm clouds gathered atop the mountains of Migdol to the south and west. No winds rushed across the calm vast surface of the Red Sea to the east. The camp quickly erupted in fear and despair when the storm's source appeared on the horizon.

Pharaoh's army of chariots was coming! Pharaoh had changed his mind, and he was in pursuit! The Jewish people cried out in dread. With mountains to the left and behind, a sea on the right, and the chariots raging toward them, they were trapped.

How could this have happened? After generations of living peaceably in Egypt, the Jewish people found themselves enslaved by Pharaoh. They worked backbreaking labor building the potentate's pyramids. They dreamed of the day they could escape to their homeland, to the land God had promised their forefathers for their inheritance.

That dream became reality when God led Moses to demand that Pharaoh set the Jewish people free. After a series of repeated demands and a series of increasingly devastating plagues, Pharaoh finally relented, releasing the Jewish slaves. Under the God-following leadership of Moses, the Jewish people prepared to leave their captor's land to make their way home.

The Jewish people gathered for their exodus out of Egypt. Families and tribes organized to make the trek home. They packed their possessions and even received a bounty of parting gifts from the Egyptians. Together, they evacuated Egypt and Pharaoh's oppression, bearing eastward toward the land promised to them. Truly, God had blessed the Jewish people, and liberty—while still a long journey away—was in sight.

Then, the unthinkable happened. Pharaoh changed his mind. Not long after he watched the Jewish population leave his mighty city—and in the shadow of his rage-filled grief over the death of his heir—Pharaoh called in his armies and commanded a pursuit. His military would hunt down the Jewish slaves, and he would reestablish his ownership.

Now, with nowhere to flee, with no cover to hide, the Jewish nation watched in peril as Pharaoh's chariots bore down upon them. They cried out in dread, because they had nowhere to turn! All they could see was a thundering army and their own inevitable death.

Keep yourselves in the love of God, looking for
the mercy of our Lord Jesus Christ
unto eternal life.

Jude 1:21 NKJV

Take a closer look at Moses' reply to the Jewish people's cries and see that while his military advice looked suicidal, it was exactly what they needed to see God's solution to their predicament. Israel's tribes were literally stuck between a rock (Migdol's mountains) and a hard place (the Red sea). In peril, they panicked.

Moses, however, reminds them, "Do not be afraid!" They were terrified because of what they could see—the chariots of Pharaoh. Moses told them to find their solution in what they could not see—the mighty hand of God. Moses commanded them to do exactly the opposite of what human logic dictates. In telling them to trust in the miracle of God that they were about to witness, he said to them, "Stand there and see what God will do!"

Moses put all his hope and trust in God. He told them to watch what God was going to accomplish; when it was all over, there would be no evidence of the Egyptian forces. He encouraged them to let the Lord fight the battle that they could not. Their responsibility was to simply hold their peace.

With that, God parted the waters of the Red Sea and provided a way.

> The Chinese use two brush strokes to write the word "crisis." One brush stroke stands for danger; the other for opportunity. In a crisis, be aware of the danger—but recognize the opportunity.
>
> Richard M. Nixon

People naturally panic when all they see is bad. Maybe the doctor called with bad news. Maybe the bank has just sent notice that your last five checks bounced, you mailed out three bills, and payday is still eight days away. Maybe you have been downsized at work and the car just broke down. Maybe you came home to find that your spouse has given up and left for a fresh start.

Apply It
to Your Life

Just like the Jewish nation, what you see can blind you with fear. When you lift your eyes and can see nothing that gives you hope, it is easy to forget that God has brought you to this place for the very purpose that you would trust him. The very worst thing you could do in impossible situations is to take matters into your own hands once more.

In the face of desperate circumstances, God wants you to hold your peace and let him fight the battle for you. He still wants you to trust him for your way out of impossible situations and watch the miracle he has planned for you. God still says, "Stand there and see what God will do!"

And he will deliver you.

Your way was through the sea, your path through the great waters; yet your footprints were unseen. You led your people like a flock by the hand of Moses and Aaron.

Psalm 77:19–20 ESV

When other people are looking to you for leadership through seemingly impossible difficulties, your determination to trust God will reshape their understanding of the Lord. Stephen J. Binz, in *The God of Freedom and Life: A Commentary on the Book of Exodus,* said:

"Moses is patient with his people this time and responds with words of encouragement and hope. 'Fear not' is the encouragement to trust in the power of God being made manifest. The 'victory' that Moses assures the people that God will win is the Hebrew word for 'salvation.' . . . They are challenged to begin shaping their vision according to their experience of freedom rather than the bondage they so painfully remember."

This new vision of freedom is fully realized for people today in the deliverance provided by Jesus upon the cross. Fleming Rutledge in *Help My Unbelief* said:

"The God who parts the waters of the Red Sea . . . appears to take the part of the refugees, to defend the defenseless, to come alongside those who suffer and to make their case his own. There is nothing like this in 'religion.' . . . This comes to its climax two thousand years later on a hill outside Jerusalem where . . . God allows himself, as Bonhoeffer wrote, to be 'pushed out of the world onto the cross' for those who have been sentenced to death."

Zooming **In**

The mountain wall of Migdol penned in the tribes of Israel to the south and west. The name Migdol means "tower," and the rocky peaks were historically used by the pharaohs' armies as a strategic location in defending the Egyptian homeland from invading armies from the east.

With provocative and controversial discoveries found as recently as 2003 of possible chariot wheels in coral reef beds (that flourish where there is an abundance of decomposing organic material, such as would be present in the drowned and defeated armies of Pharaoh), the Red Sea exploration draws countless scientists, adventure seekers, and Bible students every year.

Often, people trust in God only for deliverance as a final option, after every other option failed. Today, look up and see the victory God will accomplish for you!

Through the
Eyes of
Your Heart

Think about a time when you were desperate and feeling trapped. What were the situations that penned you in, frantic for a way out?

_____

_____

_____

_____

Did you make matters worse by taking your rescue into your own hands? If so, why did your attempt fail?

_____

_____

_____

What is the most frightening aspect of standing and waiting on God for deliverance? What tempts you to give up on God?

_____

_____

_____

_____

Frightening Insanity

The people went out to see what had happened; and they came to Jesus, and found the man from whom the demons had gone out, sitting down at the feet of Jesus, clothed and in his right mind; and they became frightened.

Luke 8:35 NASB

The Big Picture

At night, his pain-filled screams split the air and pierced the calm of the Gadarene region. As he trolled the burial grounds each night, naked except for dragging chains that had once futilely attempted to shackle him, he tore his flesh with his own fingernails and growled wildly.

People knew him as the Gadarene demoniac, and they feared him. He could not be controlled, so the people had just learned to coexist with him. They stayed out of his way and hoped he would stay out of theirs. He was dangerous, so they put up with him in order not to have to meet up with him.

News had just come in, though, that something frightening had happened. The local pig farmers ran through the streets, screaming hysterically that their pigs had rushed off a cliff and drowned in the lake below. They shouted about the demoniac, and the townspeople were likely not surprised he had something to do with it. As the details fit together, something was going on that demanded their attention.

take a CLOSER look

The man named Jesus, whom they had been hearing about, had confronted the Gadarene demoniac. Jesus had a reputation as a holy man and a miracle worker, but surely not even he was a match for the demon-filled man who roamed their region's hills. The man had been possessed by demons for longer than they could remember, and no one had been able to free him from this spiritual oppression. He was known as "Legion," in deference to the many tormentors torturing him. If ever there was a man who was beyond help, it was he.

The people of Gadarene rushed to the hills to see what had taken place in the showdown between Jesus and Legion. They steeled their nerves to witness the unknown. What carnage awaited them? Would they have to clean up Legion's destruction? Would they have to cower in fear for what Jesus may have set off in Legion? Why could he not have just let this violent man suffer his misery in solitude? They had not called for his help, and now their dysfunctional peace had been upset.

While they were prepared for the worst because of the news of their pigs' bizarre mass suicide, they were shocked and frightened by the unimaginable sight that awaited them.

Legion was calm. He was clothed. He sat at the feet of Jesus, in his right mind.

God cannot give us a happiness and peace
apart from Himself, because it is not there.
There is no such thing.

C. S. Lewis

Take a closer look at the miracle cure of the Gadarene demoniac and see that the peace-bringing power of God can be frightening. In a world desensitized to violence and brutality, when God demonstrates his might by calming a chaotic person, onlookers may be shaken by what they see.

The Gadarenes were comfortably dread-filled by the local demon-possessed man. As long as they stayed out of his way, they did not care what commotion he caused. After his encounter with Jesus, this same man who had once terrified the community was seemingly new and different because he was clothed and under control. They could not have predicted these conditions. Accordingly, they did not know how to react.

In seeing a cured demoniac, they observed the power of God. They had heard the stories of dozens of the pigs unexplainably jumping off the cliff to their death. That was a little spooky. However, they were especially frightened at the prospect of what he could do with the messes in their own lives. If Jesus could do so much with a man such as the demoniac, what changes would he work in them? That was the prospect that really scared them.

I rest beneath the Almighty's shade, my griefs expire, my troubles cease; thou, Lord, on whom my soul is stayed, wilt keep me still in perfect peace.

Charles Wesley

God continues to show his power over the controlling forces in life. If you have hidden habits, an angry spirit, or even out-of-control problems, God is able to step into your life and bring peace over all your conflicts. There is no adversary or obstacle equal to God. There are only people with problems who either trust God by faith or flee from him by fear.

God offers the blessings of peace, patience, and self-control to people in need of these blessings. He alone calms a person from the inside out. He alone provides tranquillity to replace—not cover—the turmoil.

Like the demoniac, people most in need of serenity have lives marked by conflict, anger, pain, and even destruction. God takes no delight in your misery. It is the nature of God to seek you out and bring peace to you amid your problems. If you are troubled, God invites you to "sit at his feet" in calm and comfort.

God regularly shows his power in ways that extinguish danger, violence, and conflict. These radical displays of love, while unsettling to some, are proof that God's will is good, and his ways restore you to wholeness.

When my heart was sad and I was angry, I was senseless and stupid. I acted like an animal toward you. But I am always with you; you have held my hand. You guide me with your advice, and later you will receive me in honor.

Psalm 73:21–24 NCV

Dysfunctional behavior can have roots in chemical, behavioral, physical, and spiritual abnormalities. Christ offers hope, peace, and calm regardless of the circumstance. In *Jesus and the Christian*, T. W. Manson wrote:

"When we look at history, what we see is often not merely the impersonal and unmeaning but the irrational and *the mad*. . . . Certainly, as Jesus looked at people, he saw them not always as rational moral units or self-contained autonomous spirits; he saw their souls as a battle ground, an arena or theater of tragic conflict between the opposed cosmic powers of the Holy Spirit and God and Satan."

Accordingly, you have a choice in how to respond to Jesus when he offers to bring you spiritual wholeness. Greg Laurie, in *Breakfast with Jesus,* said:

"I admit that Jesus may be bad for business but he is *great* for the soul. He can deliver you from anything—not only from a miserable past, but also from present sins, whatever they may be. He can and will do that, unless you do what the Gadarenes did and send him away."

Zooming In

People of Jesus' time disagreed about who he was. Was he a priest, a prophet, a political revolutionary, or even a reincarnated long-dead prophet? The demons possessing the afflicted man, though, had no disagreement or confusion. In fearful reverence, they identified him as "Son of God," recognizing that he was no mere man. In Jesus, they saw God, and they were afraid.

The demons identified themselves as "Legion." This name refers to a Roman military regiment, a contingent of 4,000–6,000 foot soldiers. This name reveals two important insights. First, the Gadarene victim was seriously afflicted by spiritual oppression. Second, the demonic forces in the world consider themselves at war against God. With a single command, though, they flee in an obedient response to Jesus.

While you may not be able to identify with being possessed by spiritual tormentors, you may be like the many people who have been completely incapacitated or controlled by a problem or trouble. For you, Jesus offers hope.

Take a few moments and jot down the matters that weigh down your spirit or seem to control you. How do these issues make your life feel out of control?

Do you see other people around you accommodating and adjusting uncomfortably to account for your mood, temper, or volatile personality? How has instability in your life affected others?

What would your life be like if God invaded your being, bringing peace, comfort, and stability? Does the prospect of serenity comfort or frighten you?

Building Inspection

Anyone who hears and obeys these teachings of mine is like a wise person who built a house on solid rock. Rain poured down, rivers flooded, and winds beat against that house. But it did not fall, because it was built on solid rock. Anyone who hears my teachings and doesn't obey them is like a foolish person who built a house on sand. The rain poured down, the rivers flooded, and the winds blew and beat against that house. Finally, it fell with a crash.

Matthew 7:24–27 CEV

The
Big Picture

From the side of the gently sloping mountain, Jesus preached with passion. He had pronounced blessing after blessing upon the poor, the meek, the heavy-hearted. He had taught authoritatively on prayer, temptation, and a wide range of other matters. He shared truths about God that highlighted God's gracious nature. He also repeatedly mentioned God's holiness. He encouraged the massive audience sprawled across the plain before him who had gathered expressly to receive this teacher's message. By every measure, the sermon was a success.

Jesus closed his message by painting a word picture. This was not unusual, because even on this day he had compared God's children to salt and light, God himself to a kind boss, selfish criticism to having a ridiculously large splinter in one's own eye, and a variety of other visually memorable comparisons. He concluded by comparing a wise person who obeyed the teachings he had just shared to a man who built a waterfront home safely founded in the rock bed, and disobedience to a foolish man who built a similar home, but instead tried vainly to anchor his foundation in the shifting sands.

The analogy was obvious: when the inevitable tide came rushing in, the wise man's house stood firm and the foolish man's home crashed to ruins. Obedience to God anchors a life in the stable assurance of his presence and provision, and disobedience leaves a life to risk the destructive storms that bring ruin.

Doubtless, the multitudes nodded their heads in agreement, even as they pondered the message's nuances and implications. Certainly, many people left the mountainside convinced. As they departed for home, most people likely felt encouraged for the first time in years, feeling closer to God than probably ever before. They had been given a clear word on how and what to say when they talked to God in prayer, rather than simply trusting a temple priest to intercede for them. They were told that their long-suffering would be rewarded in heaven. They were encouraged to forgive freely, because God himself offers forgiveness. They were exhorted to live in purity, in holiness, without compromise. They went home with new excitement because they had heard a fresh word from Jesus of Nazareth. They went home with a firm resolve, ready to obey.

Little did they know that in his final illustration, Jesus also issued an advance warning about an impending storm.

The purpose of problems is to push you toward obedience to God's laws, which are exact and cannot be changed. We have the free will to obey them or disobey them. Obedience will bring harmony, disobedience will bring you more problems.

Mildred Norman Ryder

Take a Closer Look

A closer look at the final exhortation of Christ's Sermon on the Mount shows that the tidal waves of life come crashing upon all people, whether wise or foolish. The only way to survive and thrive amid the inevitable tide is to live by obedience and trust.

A rabbi named Harold Kushner once wrote a book titled *When Bad Things Happen to Good People*. The book's title asks a question that every person asks in one form or another when faced with difficulty: Why me?

Jesus gives a definitive answer in his word picture about the coming tide. Simply stated, that is what life is all about. God never promises that "good people" will be free from tough times. In fact, God uses the crashing waves of calamity to reveal what truly makes a person good.

The point of Christ's Sermon on the Mount is that every life faces ebb and flow. When the waters have receded and the sun is shining, it is easy to believe God. Yet, when the waters rise and stormy situations roll relentlessly against your foundation of faith, your only hope to prevail is by steadfastly obeying God and his Word.

> *Few delights can equal the mere presence of one whom we trust utterly.*
>
> George MacDonald

Look at your own life's journey, and you can likely identify the peaks and valleys that you have alternately celebrated atop and persevered through. The same is true for all people, regardless of your opinion of them. Great people have lousy moments in life, and lousy people have great moments.

Apply It
to Your Life

The words of Christ are much more than just an encouragement to follow good advice. In fact, his good advice is that you embrace the reality that life does promise ups and downs, and the only way to survive and thrive through the low points is by completely trusting God in all life's matters. The only way to demonstrate trust is through obedience.

In this respect, the commands and encouragements of his mountaintop sermon are even more pointed and important. They are the pillars that anchor your life in the bedrock of faith. Christ will prove himself consistently whenever a storm front approaches. When you live a life defined by obedience to God, you do not have to batten down the hatches in preparation for the storm. By virtue of obedience, you already have.

What about those eighteen people who died when the tower in Siloam fell on them? Do you think they were worse than everyone else in Jerusalem? Not at all!

Luke 13:4–5 CEV

Jesus' statement comparing obedience to building on a strong foundation is the illustration that compares the difference between simply listening and actually doing. The Reverend Charles Roydon of Bedford, England, said:

"Jesus knew about building, he was a carpenter. So he used an illustration about building houses to try and draw attention to the laziness of human nature. He knew how easy it is to hear things, listen to them, agree with them and then go out and do not one thing about them. And so He told the story to show the necessity of doing as well as hearing. It is not enough to know; it is not enough to agree. Every word is given that we may use it, put it into action and make it a part of the structure as we build a life."

Bob Deffinbaugh in *The Fatal Failures of Religion* adds:

"Here is the bottom line. Here is what distinguishes true Christianity from every other religion—its foundation, its ultimate source of authority . . . the foundation upon which one builds his life is not tested until the great storm comes. We will not learn the folly of choosing the wrong gate, the wrong guide, or the wrong foundation until it is too late to reverse our destiny."

Zooming In

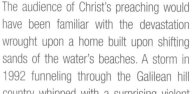

The audience of Christ's preaching would have been familiar with the devastation wrought upon a home built upon shifting sands of the water's beaches. A storm in 1992 funneling through the Galilean hill country whipped with a surprising violent effectiveness across the sea's waters and severely damaged shoreline communities.

The Gospels of Matthew and Luke appear to disagree whether the Sermon on the Mount took place on a hillside or upon a plain, but the problem is easily reconciled when viewing the commonly accepted location for Jesus' epic teaching. Once known as Mount Arbel, located between Capernaum and Tabgha, this hill outcrops from an expansive plain that could easily accommodate thousands of worshipers.

Like a sudden thunderstorm giving way to the emerging sunshine, all bad times eventually pass and hope returns. Until your unpleasant situation goes by, though, obeying God by faith is your only true shelter to keep you safe.

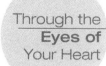

Through the
Eyes of
Your Heart

Have you ever been surprised by a thunderstorm and found yourself completely soaked? Did you do anything wrong to deserve that situation? What has been a "surprise thunderstorm" that you have experienced in your life?

_____

_____

_____

Think of areas of your life you have trusted to God and how he has proven himself faithful to you. Now, what is one area where you are disobedient? What keeps you from trusting God in that area?

_____

_____

_____

Disobedience is like having a house with a foundation weakened by the tide's relentless pounding. There is no such thing as partial obedience. How is your life strengthened by being more obedient?

_____

_____

_____

The Recipe to a Happy Life

Always be joyful. Keep on praying. No matter what happens, always be thankful, for this is God's will for you who belong to Christ Jesus.

1 Thessalonians 5:16–18 NLT

The Big Picture

When the apostle Paul wrote to the church in Thessalonica about how to live happily, they gave his words great merit. As the leader who started the church in their region, he had traveled a difficult path through their midst. Earlier, Paul and his friend Silas had been arrested there for their efforts at starting the church. Paul had preached about Jesus in the synagogue in Thessalonica on three separate occasions. This angered some of the people in the synagogue, and by the time of his third sermon, those who opposed him started a riot. They petitioned the Roman authorities to arrest Paul and Silas, but the two had already moved on to Berea, where they continued their ministry.

In the shadow of the well-known exploits of Paul, the emerging community of Christ followers received his letter with great expectation. He wrote with authority and encouragement. His wise counsel would provide direction and structure for the growing number of new Christians in the region. They happily received his letter. In turn he used this letter to teach them how to be continuously joyful.

His history of persecution and imprisonment made his prescriptive list of how to have a happy life even more profound and impacting. If anyone had a reason to be bitter or resentful, it was Paul. In his travels around the world spreading the message of God's love, Paul had been beaten with rods, whipped, robbed, shipwrecked, starved, stripped naked, and imperiled more times than could be counted. Despite this, he still spoke with a deep, abiding love for his persecutors and countrymen. He was a man who took his own advice and was able to live happily in all circumstances.

Paul's joy is transparent. Throughout his letter to the church in Thessalonica, he practically abounds with happiness. He rejoices that people are coming to faith in Jesus as the Lord and that the church is growing. He positively affirms that his ministry and their experiences with him were times that had been ordained by God for good purposes. He joyfully clears up matters of theology, including the triumphant news of Christ's imminent return. And then he offers the formula for a happy life.

God's will is for you to be happy. In giving you this recipe, he is showing how a happy life is created.

When unhappy, one doubts everything;
when happy, one doubts nothing.

Joseph Roux

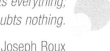

Take a closer look at the recipe for a happy life and see that Paul's plan is not a cafeteria menu. Just as the finest, smoothest chocolate cake is inedible if the sugar is withheld from the batter, a good life cannot be a truly happy life if any one of the spiritual ingredients mentioned in this passage is withheld.

Each spiritual ingredient stands on its own merit, and each will bring some measure of happiness. A person who prays consistently will likely hear from God. If that person leaves gratitude out of his life's recipe, he can eventually become bitter when life does not go as he thinks it should. A person who pursues joy but rarely prays, on the other hand, may find herself smiling on the outside but dying on the inside. Only when you persistently and consistently combine joy, prayer, and gratitude can you receive the sum measure of happiness.

Moreover, each aspect of happy living is interdependent. Prayer is essential to finding joy in life's trials. Gratitude is the expression in which that discovered joy is communicated. A commitment to living happily is a comprehensive determination to be positive and believe the best in God and in others in all circumstances and situations.

> *The Constitution only guarantees the American people the right to pursue happiness. You have to catch it yourself.*
>
> Benjamin Franklin

You cannot just throw a recipe's ingredients together in a bowl and expect to have a perfect result. You have to create your concoction with order and intentionality. The same is true for creating a truly happy life. Joy, prayer, and gratitude do not occur by accident. They must be pursued.

Rather than griping when a bad situation happens, look for opportunities to express gratitude to God for what you have learned and for how you have grown. Rather than expecting the worst when faced with a challenge, joyfully hope for the best and expect a blessing. Rather than relying on yourself or keeping problems to yourself, go to God in prayer and share with him.

Just as salt brings flavor by reducing bitterness and just as baking powder is a necessary ingredient to get baked goods to rise, so too are these spiritual ingredients elemental to a happy life. As you pursue joy, you will catch it more and more frequently. As you commit to being grateful, you will discover more reasons to actually be grateful. When you live your life according to the recipe of happiness, you will find that life is indeed sweet!

You reveal the path of life to me; in Your presence is abundant joy; in Your right hand are eternal pleasures.

Psalm 16:11 HCSB

Happiness is not just a state of mind; it is a conscientious life decision. Marcia Taylor Thompson said in *Help! I Am Leading a Children's Sermon*:

"Paul's lesson for the church in Thessalonica and for us is that everything we do is to be an act of worship toward God. Sometimes we try to separate our lives and only include God in certain areas. As we prepare to celebrate Jesus . . . we should rejoice, pray, and thank God in all we do, say, and think."

This new perspective helps develop a new perspective of gratitude in observing the world around you. Ruth Herzer said in *Warriors in Praise*:

"Paul sandwiches prayer between rejoicing and thanksgiving. Paul's praying was not begging and pleading with God. Rather he rejoiced in the benefits and blessings of the New Covenant and thanked and praised the Lord for making them real in the lives of saints. . . . Paul makes a point to mention thanksgiving along with prayer. It was definitely a characteristic of his intercession."

Zooming **In**

The city of Thessalonica, now called Thessaloniki in Macedonia, offers few archaeological discoveries because the modern city has been built upon its ancient structures. In fact, little of the local history speaks to the work and ministry of the apostle Paul, but instead glorifies the exploits of Alexander the Great, whose brother-in-law, Cassander, founded the city in 315 BC.

Thessalonica considered itself a cosmopolitan city where a person could choose to worship Isis, Serapis, Osiris, or Mithra. Abandoning these gods for the true living God was not only a willful decision to turn away from religious cults, but also a conscientious choice not to take part in the numerous trade cults where many friendships and commerce relationships developed.

It has been said that misery loves company, but company does not reciprocate. The more you fill your life with the ingredients of happiness, the fuller your life will be in every way.

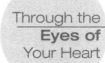

Through the
Eyes of
Your Heart

Happiness does not equate to being pain-free. How can you see the aspects of happy living in this passage helping you work through difficult times?

_____

_____

_____

If happiness is a discipline, there will be parts of your life that will make joy, gratitude, and prayer more difficult to experience. What are those areas in your life? What makes these areas difficult?

_____

_____

Some people accuse others who are consistently happy of being out of touch or fake. How can you see life in a new reality by conscientiously pursuing happiness?

_____

_____

_____

The Life-Driven Purpose

Jesus said to them again, "Truly, truly, I say to you, I am the door of the sheep. All who came before Me are thieves and robbers, but the sheep did not hear them. I am the door; if anyone enters through Me, he will be saved, and will go in and out and find pasture. The thief comes only to steal and kill and destroy; I came that they may have life, and have it abundantly."

John 10:7–10 NASB

The Big Picture

The Pharisees moved in like crime scene investigators. The crime was obvious: a man who had been blind since birth now had sight. A miracle had happened here; to make matters worse, it was performed on the Sabbath. The Law had been broken, and the Pharisees were on the scene to find the culprit. They asked the once-blind man's friends and neighbors to determine if he really had been, in fact, blind. They had to rule out fraud. The reluctant witnesses all agreed that the man was real, as was his blindness. The Pharisees were thorough, bringing in his parents to see if the man was really their son and if he really had been healed. The investigators had such a harsh reputation that even the parents were unwilling to put themselves at risk for the healed man. They refused to incriminate themselves and left the young man to his own defense.

Ultimately, the Pharisees could not discredit the miracle. The lawmen then turned their attention to the miracle giver, this man named Jesus. They began grilling the newly sighted man, poking and prodding for evidence

take a **CLOSER** look

against Jesus. The witness was little help. He did not know where to find Jesus. He did not know where he was from. All he knew was that Jesus had made clay by mixing spit with dirt, rubbed it on the blind man's eyes, and the blind man suddenly had sight for the first time in his life!

Jesus soon heard news of the investigation and found the man he had recently healed. Hoping to capture their suspect if he returned to the scene, the Pharisees hid poised nearby. They quickly pounced, confronting Jesus when they overheard him virtually confessing.

The Pharisees had their evidence, but they still needed motive. So they asked Jesus a leading question.

Here, Jesus turned the tables on the Pharisees, showing that he knew their laws even better than they did themselves. He compared them to wolves who devour innocent sheep and contrasted himself as both the good shepherd who protects the sheep and the gate by which the sheep find safe pasture. Then, in defiant confidence, he confessed the purpose behind his miraculous works, explaining, "I came that they may have life, and have it abundantly"!

Let each man think himself an act of God, his mind a thought, his life a breath of God; and let each try, by great thoughts and good deeds, to show the most of Heaven he hath in him.

Philip James Bailey

A closer look at the confession of Jesus shows that while the rest of the world spends life searching vainly for purpose, he came to show that his entire purpose is to give life to the world. Since time began, people have been asking themselves, each other, and even God, "Why am I here?" Solomon, in the book of Ecclesiastes, explains in painstaking detail the frustrating discoveries of all the dead-end answers he discovered in search of an answer to this question. Heroes of faith—stalwarts like Moses and Ruth of the Old Testament and Peter and John the Baptist—had times of doubt. Even today, millions of people spend tens of millions of dollars on well-written books that address the question "What is my purpose in life?"

Jesus is the one person in human history who never questioned or doubted his purpose. Three times Satan tried to derail him from his purpose of bringing life to the world. The Bible mentions numerous people who tried to distract Jesus from this purpose because they thought he would make a great priest, or a prophet, or even a king. Jesus' entire purpose was to bring life, a gift found only in him.

> *Jesus loves me, this I know, for the Bible tells me so.*
>
> Karl Barth
>
> author of the twelve-volume work *Church Dogmatics*, on being asked the most important theological truth he knew

Imagine picking up a shiny red apple, perfect in color and shape, and taking a bite, only to find out that it was made of wax.

Too many people live wax-fruit lives. These people's lives look great, but everything that is good and impressive is just on the surface. Underneath wealth, possessions, or experiences, they are really hurting and empty.

Jesus left the riches of heaven to bring you life. The life that Jesus brings is not about having outward riches that impress other people. The life Jesus brings is discovered in the internal blessings that fill your life richly. Jesus offers life redefined in terms of both quality and quantity of experiences and understanding.

Jesus came to give life "abundantly." That means you will still face the peaks and valleys of life, but you will face them with him. He will provide you peace, joy, contentment, hope, and expectation as you pass through trials and triumphs. He will provide you with everything you need for this life, as well as for the life that follows death. By receiving him as life, you will spend eternity with God in heaven. The life-filled purpose of Jesus offers a purpose-filled life for you!

You are my friends when you do the things I command you.

John 15:14 MSG

The more you understand the concept of abundant life, the more you will recognize the abundance of blessings God bestows in its expression. Peter J. Gomes said in *Strength for the Journey*:

"For Jesus, abundance is fullness—that is, the lack and absence of anxiety, fear, or terror, for those things have been driven out by peace, joy, and love. The abundant life of which our Lord speaks with special reference to his sheep has more to do with security than prosperity. It is dangerous for a sheep to be fat and complacent and unable to move quickly, and the shepherd vows to protect it from itself and from everything and from everybody else."

R. Paul Olson, in *The Reconciled Life: A Critical Theory of Counseling*, said:

"The abundant life Jesus described is not primarily a material life. It is a spiritual blessing. Abundant living is a matter affecting the whole person. . . . The term 'life' suggests that I experience God's gift of abundant living as a whole person. . . . The abundant life is a spiritual life with God that lasts beyond the limits of finite time."

Zooming **In**

The Greek word for compassion—*splanchnizomai*—often explains what motivated Jesus to perform a healing miracle. This word's root literally means "spleen" or "intestines." Using this root word is comparable to using the word *guts* to mean "courage" in modern English. This same courageous compassion compelled Jesus to leave heaven to bring life to the people of the world.

Before declaring his life-driven purpose, Jesus explained that he was both "the good shepherd" and "the gate." In New Testament times, shepherds created makeshift sheep pens from large rocks and briarwoods. The shepherd would then lie down at the opening of these pens, serving as the gate that any predator would have to cross to attack the flock.

Understanding Jesus' purpose to bring you real life can shape your own life's purpose. This is the difference between a dead-end life and a life with a destination in sight.

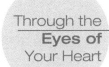

Through the
Eyes of
Your Heart

What are some dead ends you have discovered in searching for purpose in life? What did you think about God when you hit those dead ends?

_____

_____

_____

_____

Sometimes people misunderstand a gift, not knowing its purpose. In the past, how have you misunderstood the gift of Jesus? How did that misunderstanding cause you to be unsatisfied with God?

_____

_____

_____

How would life be different if you redefined "quality of life" according to Jesus' standard instead of your own?

_____

_____

_____

_____

Internal Medicine

> *[If] My people who are called by My name humble themselves, pray and seek My face, and turn from their evil ways, then I will hear from heaven, forgive their sin, and heal their land.*
>
> 2 Chronicles 7:14 HCSB

The Big Picture

Finally, the temple of God was complete. The kingdom of Israel celebrated under the leadership of King Solomon, because they now had a glorious house of worship constructed to exacting specifications. It was resplendent in its majesty; truly it embodied the splendor of God himself.

The dedication of the temple was no small celebration, either. With tremendous and altogether worthy fanfare, the Levite priests had followed the Ark of the Covenant into the temple. The Lord God himself filled the temple in the form of a cloud, and the ministers trumpeted his presence in praise and adoration.

Then, King Solomon came forward and stood before the assembly of all the rejoicing-but-solemn worshipers, and he dedicated the temple unto the Lord and offered a humble, heartfelt prayer where he extolled the faithfulness of God and implored the Lord's continued blessing, leading, and favor.

In any other place, and at any other time, this momentous celebration would have climaxed at the pronouncement of the king. God showed up and reminded everybody that he was the object of their worship. Fire from heaven blazed down and consumed their sacrificial offerings. People fell to their faces in worship. The sacrifices were offered, and the people feasted for seven days and nights.

On the eighth day, in the quiet of his own private sleeping quarters, King Solomon reflected in amazement on all that had just taken place. In the calm of this moment, God once again appeared and spoke a word to Solomon that still rings in the ears of God-fearing nations today.

He reminded Israel's king and believers today that he is the giver and with-holder of blessings. And if people will commit to putting God first, they will experience blessing. He alone will forgive them, and he alone will heal them. He alone will make a people—or a nation—whole.

In the centuries that have followed this genuine promise, this Scripture has been used both to indicate the guilt of nations that have turned their back upon God and to warn other nations not to do the same. It has been used as an explanation for why Christian nations act no better than non-Christian nations and as an appeal for godly behavior. In all these expressions, God's promise holds invariably firm. The blessing waits.

There is no justification without sanctification, no forgiveness without renewal of life, no real faith from which the fruits of new obedience do not grow.

Martin Luther

A closer look at God's clear exhortation to King Solomon shows that revival is dependent upon the change of heart of God's people alone. This verse is invoked every time a call is raised for a national return to seeking God. Attention here should be given, though, not just to the promises that God has made, but that his plan for healing is contingent upon God's people responding, not lost people or heathens.

People filling churches all over the world want to see their lands transformed by the presence of God. The problem is not that the unbelieving world is filled with unbelievers. It is the nature of disbelief to disbelieve. The problem is that the home of believers—the church—is filled with too much disbelief.

God has mandated that his people must turn from their wicked ways. God's people need to stop acting like they did before they followed God. The church must stop relying on itself and begin relying on God if it wants to see a heavenly blessing.

God has promised that if the church calls upon him—relies upon God utterly, in everything—he will hear the prayer and answer it, and rain down spiritual blessing that has not been seen in this lifetime.

> Mere sorrow, which weeps and sits still, is not repentance. Repentance is sorrow converted into action; into a movement toward a new and better life.
>
> M. R. Vincent

If you are one of God's people, then it is wise to rate how well you measure up to God's challenge. The first step is to humble yourself, which requires that you look at yourself honestly. Honestly assess your motives, words, attitudes, behaviors, and actions. Ask God to show you where pride has led you to do things in a spirit of independence, apart from God.

Then God prescribes the necessary medicine to cure pride. This prescription requires a change of heart that leads to a change of action. For example, if you planned to take the elevator to the top floor but you saw a sign on the door reading "Work in progress . . . back in 5 minutes," you would change your mind and actions to take the stairs. Likewise, it is even more important to change your actions to follow God so pride does not hinder God's work through your life.

God promises to answer a humble person. You will experience a new, dynamic relationship with him where you see blessings you've never before experienced, and you will see him bring healing to spiritual and relational wounds that were otherwise incurable.

If you return to the Almighty, you will be blessed again.
Job 22:23 NCV

The need for reconciliation with God is pressing because it frees you to follow God. Siang-Yang Tan said in *Disciplines of the Holy Spirit: How to Connect to the Spirit's Power and Presence*:

"Repentance and confession are the first steps into surrender. Through these disciplines, we begin to walk in humility away from the root of inward corruption centered in pride. Repentance and confession are the antidote to pride—they kill it! . . . One of the very best things we can do for growth in Christ is to cultivate for ourselves a willing spirit of repentance.

"When those who follow God return to a right relationship with him individually and corporately, they will see God accomplish feats that before they had only imagined or read about."

In *Fresh Wind, Fresh Fire,* Jim Cymbala wrote:

"The work of God can only be carried on by the power of God. The church is a spiritual organism fighting spiritual battles. Only spiritual power can make it function as God ordained. . . . Are you and I seeing the results that Peter saw? If not, we need to get back to his power source."

Zooming In

In Old Testament practice, repentance was a religious act where a person provided the Jewish high priest with an animal to be sacrificed on the temple's altar. This animal's blood was spilled as a penalty sacrifice for the offender's transgressions.

Biblical history records a circular pattern of the fulfillment of this promise of God to the people of Israel. Repeatedly, the nation's populace strayed from faithfulness to God. Consequently, they fell under the authority of godless kings. Usually under the direction of a brave prophet, they would repent and return to faith and God would heal their land and provide them with a godly leader.

Realizing God's forgiveness is a freeing experience that helps you understand God in a new, exciting way. It releases you from the traps of past mistakes so you can do great things that before seemed impossible.

It is tempting but common for a person to feel God cannot forgive a certain mistake. What is the worst mistake you have ever made? What does it feel like to trust that God is bigger than even your biggest mistake?

If you are like most people, you may mess up the same way repeatedly, even after thinking you would never make the same mistake again. How does it change your understanding of God to know that he never gives up on you, despite repeated self-inflicted setbacks?

God says he will heal you. How are your past mistakes like wounds and how will your life be different when you are no longer hindered by these wounds?

Personal Failure

> *I am the vine; you are the branches. If a man remains in me and I in him, he will bear much fruit; apart from me you can do nothing.*
>
> John 15:5 NIV

The Big Picture

For the twelve men who shared the dining table with Jesus, surely this night would stay with them for the remainder of their lives. The night began with a heated debate, but ended far differently. Arguments of greatness fell dead when they watched their Lord humble himself and begin cleaning their dusty, dirty, stinking feet.

Jesus followed this profound object lesson with encouraging words about the events he was about to face and the work that he had prepared for them to accomplish. Then, to emphasize their part in the events that would fill and fulfill the remainder of their lives, he talked gardening with his disciples.

These men were not experts in the garden, but they were familiar with its principles. In their culture and in their community, vineyards were common. Jesus used the common understanding of nurturing the fruit of the vine to illustrate how God would bring fullness to their lives.

take a CLOSER look

To a room full of frightened friends and discouraged disciples, Jesus warmly compared God to the gardener who tends to the grapevine, to himself as that vine, and to his followers as the branches on that vine. He spoke with encouragement about the work that awaited them, in terms of the fruit of the vine. He spoke of the work of God in them as the efforts of the gardener tending to the vine. He explained that if they wanted to experience everything that God had planned for them, they would have to live in full dependence upon God. They would experience times of "pruning," when they would be subjected to experiences that might seem unpleasant or difficult. Even these moments were for the disciples' good and part of God's plan. God would use these situations to bring about important growth to each of Jesus' followers, giving them wisdom and experience that they would be able to apply to future challenges and opportunities.

In illustrating this word picture, Jesus painted an image that emboldened a roomful of discouraged and wondering followers—and every subsequent generation of followers as well. Success in the important spiritual work of God is dependent upon God alone. A person's job is to simply enjoy the blessing by staying connected to the Father through the Son.

To me, to live is Christ, and to die is gain.

Philippians 1:21 NKJV

A closer look at this passage shows that absolute failure is the inevitable consequence for a person who jumps ahead of God in service. If you go on your own, God promises that not only is he not obligated to grant you blessings, but also that, specifically, you will fail. In this, even good things are not God things if done apart from Christ.

Jesus gave the example of the correct order for carrying out work done in his name. For Jesus, prayer preceded every act of ministry he conducted. Time and again, Jesus withdrew himself from the crowd so that he could pray to the Father. Then, once his time of prayer was complete, he went and engaged in successful, life-changing ministry. For Jesus, prayer was the hard work and ministry was the fulfillment of blessing of everything that had already been promised in prayer.

Today, many people have turned this procedure upside down. They put a good idea to work, and only after they have begun do they ask God to bless their effort. They are surprised and discouraged when they fail. Jesus reminds his followers that God's way is the only way that promises lasting results.

In war, when a commander becomes so bereft of reason and perspective that he fails to understand the dependence of arms on Divine guidance, he no longer deserves victory.

General Douglas MacArthur

Jesus invites you to find your life in him. With this passage, he is exhorting you not to step ahead of him, not to try to do anything that God has not first told you to do. God wants you to succeed. He wants you to see spiritual blessings. He wants it so much that he has devised a foolproof procedure for you to follow.

Notice that Jesus talks in third person when talking about success. "If a man remains in me . . ." Jesus is promising that this plan is universally applicable. Any person and every person can see success if they follow Christ's plan.

However, Christ's attention shifts focus when he speaks about failure. He shifts from third person to second person. "Apart from me you can do nothing." He wants you to get it. He does not want you to be confused. He does not want you to think that this explanation is for everyone else. He wants you to understand that if you go out on your own, you will not succeed.

God offers an action plan that works. This plan requires trusting God solely and following Jesus wholly. This life will bear much fruit.

You didn't choose me, remember; I chose you, and put you in the world to bear fruit, fruit that won't spoil. As fruit bearers, whatever you ask the Father in relation to me, he gives you.

John 15:16 MSG

How Others
See It

To be a branch on the vine means to be in union with Christ. This union is a growing relationship, even if at times it feels no different from life prior to faith. Robin Boisvert and C. J. Mahany said in *How Can I Change?*:

"Whether or not we *feel* united with Christ is of secondary importance; the fact is, we are. This is our status as believers. Does a marriage cease to exist just because a husband and wife feel distant from each other? Of course not. . . . Feelings—or lack thereof—in no way jeopardize the fact of our union with Christ."

Ben Campbell Johnson adds in *Living Before God*:

"All my life I have been interested in being a faithful disciple. As I review my life, I see patches of shameful failure that I regret. I have practiced a variety of disciplines, devoted myself to his work, and prayed much about being a trustworthy disciple. In this text I see that all my efforts count for nothing apart from Christ. Whatever invitations I have responded to, whatever notions of the Spirit have moved me, and whatever grace that has been shown to me is all that matters. Without him, I can do nothing!"

Zooming **In**

Jesus declares, "I am the vine." The Pharisees recognized that his claim was nothing less than a definitive assertion that he was God in the flesh, because it echoes the Old Testament response God gave to Moses when the patriarch asked what he should say God's name was to those who would ask when he told them he came in the Lord's name. "I AM WHO I AM" (Exodus 3:14 NASB) was God's reply. Jesus' own "I am" statement was a claim that he was the same Lord who had answered Moses, and it was this claim that agitated the Pharisees to arrest him for blasphemy.

take a CLOSER look

If you trust in God completely, you will experience a fruitful life. If you strike out on your own, you can only expect futility.

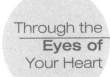

Through the
Eyes of
Your Heart

A person's nature seems to contradict Christ's assertions. How can your life's big accomplishments still be viewed as meaningless from God's perspective? How does this change the goals you set for yourself?

You may know other people who are a success based on every common measure, but they have no ongoing, close relationship with God. How does their success influence your own relationship with God?

Jesus said he will never leave or turn his back on someone who comes to him. How does this affect you? What does it mean to you to "abide in him"?

Net Worth

Passing alongside the Sea of Galilee, he saw Simon and Andrew the brother of Simon casting a net into the sea, for they were fishermen. And Jesus said to them, "Follow me, and I will make you become fishers of men."

Mark 1:16–17 ESV

The Big Picture

Simon and his brother Andrew were passionate about God. They lived in a religious culture that was full of talk about a soon-coming Messiah who would lead their people to peace and prosperity. Unfortunately for them, as fishermen, their lot in life was set before they were born. In their culture, a person's worth was established by virtue of his or her heritage. If a father was a fisherman, his sons would invariably learn the family trade and become fishermen, too. Spiritual men beget spiritual men and laborers beget laborers. There was little hope of getting out of the career path set by the preceding generations. According to their culture, they did not have the religious credentials to be part of a spiritual revolution ushering in the reign of God's Messiah. They would instead be relegated to the shores of Galilee, casting nets and harvesting schools of fish for their livelihood.

Then Jesus walked across the shores of Galilee and everything changed. He was a fresh voice in a well-established religious system. While his established counterparts were talking about the letter of the law, Jesus spoke

take a CLOSER look

about the impending kingdom of God and called upon people to seek God's forgiveness. Jesus saw Simon and Andrew faithfully plying their trade from their fishing boat and saw potential. He did not exclude them because they were dirty and smelly and uneducated. He did not think of all the reasons why they had no right to sit in spiritual authority. He looked at the brothers and determined they were the perfect candidates to help him accomplish his purpose.

So he invited them to join him in his work. In his eyes, they were worth much more than what they could pull in from their nets. He would train them. He would invest in them. He would guide their path. He would build upon the skills they had spent years learning as fishermen, and he would help them use those skills in a new way, to gather people rather than fish.

For these men, following Jesus was more than just an opportunity to learn a new trade or even to take a new direction in life. It was more than a chance to escape the life of a fisherman. Following Jesus was also their opportunity to imitate the ways, methods, and even attitudes of this rabbi. As followers of Jesus, they were now his students-in-training, appointed to reproduce what the Christ himself was doing for the benefit of others.

Love lasts when the relationship comes first.

Author Unknown

This well-known passage is often used to focus Christians upon sharing their beliefs with other people in an effort to be fishers of men. However, take a closer look at the call of Jesus and notice that he invites Simon and Andrew to join him in a relationship, not merely a new lesson on a different sort of fishing. He invites the brothers to follow him at the very time that they were casting their nets into the waters. Ironically, following Jesus meant that the brothers would have to give up the trade they knew for a new experience where they would be out of their element. Jesus invited them to leave their old world behind to go on a new adventure. While this opportunity was a chance to break free from their trade as fishermen, it was more important as a chance to know Jesus personally.

"I will make you become fishers of men," Jesus told the brothers. Jesus offered to invest himself fully in these brothers so they could accomplish the purpose he had in mind for them. As they grew to know Jesus, they would be better equipped to offer that same relationship to others. Jesus was not leaving the outcome up to their old skills as fishermen, their talents, or their abilities. He alone took responsibility for the outcome of the relationship that would develop if they followed him, and the world would never be the same.

> *I'd give it all
> for one good friend.*
>
> Howard Hughes, worth
> $4 billion at the time

Too many people today focus more on the prize of seeing someone place trust in God than in building authentic friendships with others. If a person ever feels that you care more about changing their beliefs than in developing a relationship with them, Christianity becomes nothing more than a sales pitch or a scheme. Jesus does not recruit people to be part of a sales force or even an executive team. He is calling people to follow him, extending the invitation to be his friend.

Apply It
to Your Life

By joining Jesus, you will go where he goes. This means you will have times of service, giving, and sacrifice. It also means you will do what he did—that you will pray and forgive and love and share. As you follow Jesus, you will experience what he experienced. You may be teased or mocked or maybe even ridiculed. Yet, like Jesus, you will see people drawn to God through you.

The desire to see other people have a relationship with Jesus comes from your own authentic relationship with him. Just as with Simon and Andrew, Jesus still takes the responsibility for the outcome of future expeditions. In making you a "fisher of men," Jesus will work through you to connect with others and offer them the same invitation to come alongside him.

Don't be embarrassed to speak up for our Master or for me, his prisoner. Take your share of suffering for the Message along with the rest of us. We can only keep on going, after all, by the power of God.

2 Timothy 1:8 MSG

The call to join Jesus should be understood to have far-reaching implications. R. Kent Hughes, in *Mark: Jesus, Servant and Savior,* wrote:

"Christ came with a radical message and then a radical call and these four responded in radical obedience. . . . Let us think of what their obedience meant. First, it meant an immensely expanded life. . . . In the place of Galilee came the world! . . . Peter went to Rome and Andrew went to the far borders of Russia. Their hearts were enlarged to take in the whole world. Their minds, once circumscribed and committed to the smallest interests, now overflowed with deep thoughts. They became theologians, thinkers, sociologists, psychologists, and strategists—all because of the gospel!"

William L. Lane said in *The Gospel of Mark*:

"The call to come after someone implies discipleship because it is the disciple who breaks all other ties to follow his master as servant. Yet far more than this is implied in the call to be 'fishers of men.' . . . The summons to be fishers of men is a call to the eschatological task of gathering men in view of the forthcoming judgment of God."

Zooming **In**

In biblical times, fishing with a net from a boat was very different from fishing from shore. Fishing with a net from a boat was labor-intensive and often frustratingly unsuccessful. It required knowledge about how to use the net as a tool, where in the lake to anchor, and how to repair the net when it broke. The job also required a dogged determination to keep fishing even after numerous unsuccessful casts into the sea.

While the Bible gives accounts of individuals coming to faith in Christ, it also offers many instances where multitudes came to belief in a single setting. The perseverance of early disciples showed that whether the catch was large or small, they expected and experienced results whenever they cast the "net" of God's love and forgiveness.

take a CLOSER look

Spending time with a mentor is usually more meaningful for the experience of being with that friend than it is for what you do together. You learn from your experienced friend and have a great time in the process. This is the principle Jesus offers in the invitation to join him.

Jesus is both "Lord of all" and "a friend to the friendless." Have you ever felt like you were alone and without a friend? What was that time like?

Following Jesus brings direction in life and draws others into relationship. Think of a time when you went on a journey with others. What special memories do you have of the shared experience?

What is Oprah Winfrey, Michael Jordan, or Bill Gates worth? According to Jesus, they are each worth one Savior, just like you. How does it make you feel to know that in God's economy, you are as valuable as these wealthy people?

Jesus As He Appears Today

When I turned to see who was speaking to me, I saw seven gold lampstands. And standing in the middle of the lampstands was the Son of Man. He was wearing a long robe with a gold sash across his chest. His head and his hair were white like wool, as white as snow. And his eyes were bright like flames of fire. His feet were as bright as bronze refined in a furnace, and his voice thundered like mighty ocean waves. He held seven stars in his right hand, and a sharp two-edged sword came from his mouth. And his face was as bright as the sun in all its brilliance.

Revelation 1:12–16 NLT

The Big Picture

The apostle John was an old man who treasured his memories. They comforted him in his loneliness while imprisoned on the Greek island of Patmos. He was the last living apostle; all the others had been martyred for following Jesus. John's own punishment for taking the gospel to the world was banishment here by the Roman emperor Domitian. It was here that John paged through his memories, rejoicing in the wonderful experiences and meditating upon them to glean more wisdom and truth.

The now-old follower of Christ settled into a routine to pass his days. He recalled the Scriptures that had been long-hidden in his heart. He prayed continuously, petitioning and praising and interceding for others. He remembered the brief-but-precious years he walked with his friend and Lord Jesus, marveling that he had been honored to call God's Messiah both of these titles. He did these things as worship, and this worship filled his life.

take a CLOSER look

It was in this setting of worshiping in isolation while on Patmos that John one day witnessed something that was altogether awful and awesome at the same time. It was terrifying and terrific. It was nothing short of a fresh revelation from God himself, where the Creator of all things opened the vault of time and gave this faithful servant of Jesus a vision of how this world would end and eternity would begin.

As the door to this vision opened, John fearfully turned at the command of Christ's familiar voice to withhold the unimaginable. He counted seven lampstands representing seven churches, each crafted from pure gold, and each ablaze with bright fire. Yet these lamps were suddenly and fully diminished by the appearance of Jesus.

Certainly, Jesus appeared familiar to his friend John, yet clearly he was also now altogether different. From head to toe, from voice to dress, Jesus no longer looked like the wandering rabbi. He was incredible to behold. With eyes blazing brighter than flame and hair so white it outshone the whitest white, he revealed the appearance of holiness. He looked . . . divine.

At that moment, everything that John had remembered about Jesus was redefined because he now saw Jesus as God. This is how Jesus appears today.

Do not be afraid. I am the First and the Last. I am the Living One; I was dead, and behold I am alive for ever and ever!

Revelation 1:17–18 NIV

Take a closer look at the vision of John to see Jesus as he appears today. When most people imagine the appearance of Jesus, one of two images prevails. Most often, either Jesus is thought to be the baby of the Christmas story or he is the roving rabbi of the Bible's Gospels. In fact, virtually every significant piece of artwork representing Jesus embodies him as one of these two representations. Every moment of his life retold in the Scriptures has also been captured on canvas.

However, this passage shows that the resurrected and risen Jesus is altogether different in appearance, and his visage is impressive. Pure white hair reflecting his holiness. Piercing eyes, uniquely suited to discern the heart of every person. His voice rolls like the roaring ocean; it is the voice that spoke the universe into being! His countenance is so pure, so holy, and so regal that it shines greater than the sun.

Today, Jesus appears as God, revealing his eternal glory. He is incredible and virtually indescribable. John's verbal sketch likely only begins to capture the grandeur of his image. It is no wonder that when John himself saw him, he fell on his face as though dead (Revelation 1:17).

If resurrections happened regularly, there would be nothing different about Jesus being raised from the dead. He would be one among many, just another statistic. . . . If [Jesus' resurrection] is unique, then, by definition, there will be no analogous events. That makes it a lot harder to believe. It also makes it worth believing.

Alister E. McGrath

How do you view Jesus today? If your thoughts are of a helpless baby cooing on a manger's bed of hay or of a longhaired, homeless preacher, then your mental album is not up-to-date. How you view Jesus profoundly influences how you follow Jesus. Your perception of Jesus correlates to your pursuit of Jesus.

Apply It
to Your Life

Herod Agrippa acknowledged the lordship of the baby Jesus while plotting to kill him. Religious experts debated the rabbi Jesus for three years while the entire time they plotted to crucify him. In the same way, if your view of Jesus does not reach into the heavens and see him as God, then you are only viewing Jesus in his human form. Such a perception is flawed and will lead to eventual disobedience.

It is only by viewing Jesus as he is today—as pure, holy, and perfect God—that you worship God in a manner that truly honors him. Today—and forever more—Jesus is the resurrected Lord. He is the Creator and sustainer of all things. He is God. While his image is fear-worthy, he shares this appearance of himself with you so that you will trust him with your every need and even your very life.

And on His robe and on His thigh He has a name written, "KING OF KINGS, AND LORD OF LORDS."

Revelation 19:16 NASB

Seeing Jesus as he is today will radically alter your perception of whom you worship. John Piper, in *Seeing and Savoring Jesus Christ,* said:

"The first particular glory that upholds all the rest is the mere eternal existence of Christ. If we will simply ponder this as we ought, a great ballast will come to the tipping ship of our soul. Sheer existence is, perhaps, the greatest mystery of all. Ponder the absoluteness of reality. There had to be something that never came into being. Back, back, back we peer into endless ages. Yet there was never nothing. Someone has the honor of first and always. He never became or developed. He simply was."

Marva J. Dawn concurs in *Joy in Our Weakness: A Gift of Hope from the Book of Revelation*:

"From this book we will learn what Jesus is like in all the fullness of his glorified Lordship. That vision will fill us with hope. God gave this revelation to Jesus to show the seer John what would happen so that God's people would be encouraged to trust his Lordship in all their struggles."

Zooming **In**

Revelation 1:20 explains that the seven lampstands amid which Jesus walked represent the seven churches examined in two subsequent chapters. While what the seven churches represent is the subject of much discussion, that Jesus stands amid these churches wearing a white robe with a gold band is a clear picture of his role as high priest (cf. Leviticus 24:3–4), at watch over all churches.

John's vision of Jesus is strikingly similar to the vision of "The Ancient of Days" given to Daniel in the Old Testament (Daniel 7:9–14). The consistency of the visual image, despite taking place more than six hundred years apart, offers reliable insight regarding how the eternal Lord appears in heaven. In both cases he is holy, mighty, authoritative, and victorious.

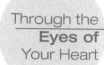

Through the
Eyes of
Your Heart

When you think about Jesus, what is the image that comes to mind? What factors influence your perception of him?

What is your reaction when you think of Jesus expressly in terms of his description in Revelation 1? Does this description of him draw you closer to him or evoke some other response? Why?

This is the real Jesus; the same Lord who created and calmed the waters, healed the lame, and wept over dead friends. How does a full understanding change how you relate to Jesus with your needs?

Filing a Petition

When Daniel learned that the law had been signed, he went home and knelt down as usual in his upstairs room, with its windows open toward Jerusalem. He prayed three times a day, just as he had always done, giving thanks to his God. The officials went together to Daniel's house and found him praying and asking for God's help.

Daniel 6:10–11 NLT

The Big Picture

Daniel, perhaps more than anyone else in the entire Old Testament, showed an amazing ability to work with others. As a young man considered among the best and brightest of all the Jewish youth, he was kidnapped and pressed into the royal service of the Babylonian king Nebuchadnezzar when the warring nation quickly took over his own. Daniel faithfully served the pagan king without compromising his own beliefs, and God honored the young man's reliable witness. The king showed favor to Daniel by elevating him to a position of authority and responsibility over all the wise men in Babylon.

Now some sixty years later, under the kingly authority of Belshazzar (the last of the Babylonian rulers), Daniel was a man of high reputation. The king called to Daniel to interpret an unexplainable supernatural experience where the king and his party saw the handwriting of God upon the wall. Daniel faithfully broke the bad news that God had judged the king, and his doom was imminent. Belshazzar honored Daniel by naming him third in power of all the land. That very night, Belshazzar was slain and the kingdom was conquered by the Persians.

take a CLOSER look

Rather than being a victim of corporate downsizing in a time of restructure, Daniel became one of three governors over 120 regional authorities, appointed by the Persian king Darius. Daniel quickly distinguished himself over his peers, and Darius began mentioning this old Jewish man as his potential right-hand man.

This infuriated his counterparts, so they plotted to bring about his demise. They attacked where they thought he was weakest—his predictable loyalty to his God. They convinced Darius to enact a law making it illegal to worship anyone but the king himself, punishable by death in a lions' den.

This conspiracy accomplished its wicked goals, or so the plotters thought. Daniel was quickly arrested for immediately violating the edict, as was predicted. Darius agonized, but ultimately capitulated to the law and had Daniel thrown into the den.

God protected Daniel from the ravenous lions, and the next morning, Darius had him withdrawn from the den. As his Babylonian predecessor Nebuchadnezzar had done decades earlier, the Persian king Darius honored God because of Daniel's faithful witness. The conspirators, consequently, became lion chow.

Under several pagan kings, Daniel prospered. He never compromised his integrity or his devotion to the Lord. His refusal to bow under pressure—even under great personal risk—brought great honor and distinction.

If you have integrity, nothing else matters. If you do not have integrity, nothing else matters.

Alan K. Simpson

Take a
Closer Look

Look carefully at Daniel's response to the laws forbidding restricting his worship. Notice that he did not complain. He did not try to combat the legislation. He did not rally a protest. He simply did what he always did. He just went home that very day and prayed to God three times, giving thanks. As the passage clearly points out, *this was his custom*.

For years, Daniel had established a pattern of living that put God first, no matter the consideration. When he was young, he refused to indulge in pagan foods offered to false gods. When he was older, he boldly spoke God's judgment upon the Babylonian king, even at the risk of his own life. For Daniel, spiritual compromise was a bigger danger than pleasing others with false words and empty promises.

Daniel stood tall and did right regardless of the risk because he refused to betray his Lord. Daniel had simply seen God prove himself too many times throughout the years to compromise his faith. In the face of a law that demanded his death, Daniel simply went to his prayer room and filed a petition with the author of divine law. God honored Daniel because Daniel faithfully honored God.

> *To give real service you must add something which cannot be bought or measured with money, and that is sincerity and integrity.*
>
> Douglas Adams

Many times in life, you will be pressed either to put God first or to set him aside. It may be a small, seemingly insignificant choice, or something so big that it could change how you worship God. Daniel's example has shown that, large or small, decisions you make tomorrow are determined by customs you establish as your life patterns today.

Apply It
to Your Life

With this in mind, the patterns you establish are formed by the integrity of your priorities. For Daniel, God was first in his life in every situation and in every circumstance. Daniel saw spiritual compromise and moral corruption all around him, yet refused to join in. God rewarded Daniel's integrity by always meeting his needs, particularly in the times when Daniel could not get out of a tough situation without God.

Like Daniel, traps are waiting all around you, specifically to betray your faith. There will constantly be temptations to turn your back on what God wants and what you know to be right. Daniel demonstrated that keeping God at the top of your priorities will sometimes put you in a jam. He also showed that keeping God at the top of your priorities is the only way to get out of a jam.

Likewise, exhort the young men to be sober-minded, in all things showing yourself to be a pattern of good works; in doctrine showing integrity, reverence, incorruptibility, sound speech that cannot be condemned, that one who is an opponent may be ashamed, having nothing evil to say of you.

Titus 2:6–8 NKJV

Integrity in the heat of trouble, while always risky, is also its own reward. Consider what Henrietta Mears said in *What the Bible Is All About*:

"Daniel's conduct in the face of danger was quite deliberate. He knew he had to deny his religion or be prepared to die for it. There was nothing different in his actions. He prayed as was his custom. His actions would influence the other Jews. By drawing attention to himself, he might reduce the danger for others. Daniel's faith during this ordeal was glorious and what we would expect from a man ripened from years with God."

Marvin Olasky, who builds on this premise in *Standing for Christ in a Modern Babylon,* said:

"Christians, of course, face pressure to appease the Babylonians. A forthright Christian student taking a test or writing a term paper for an adversarial professor has to count the cost. He may be graded down for taking a stand for Christ. . . . Whether we are presenting the gospel or a Bible-based political position, we should search out points of contact, fighting hard but fighting smart. We should learn about our Babylonian culture, as Daniel did his. But whether we are stand-up Christians or stand-up comics depends upon whose applause we covet."

Zooming **In**

The name Daniel means "Judge of God." Nebuchadnezzar had him renamed Belteshazzar in an attempt to remove the young man's essential identity from association with the God of his youth. Daniel was likely unsurprised by this attack on his personhood. As a student of the Hebrew Scriptures prior to being taken hostage by the Babylonians, Daniel would have been familiar with the patriarchal exploits of his ancestor Joseph, who had been renamed Zaphenath-paneah by the Egyptian pharaoh. Yet, by the time the accounts of his life are recorded in the sixth chapter, he is only referred to as Daniel. God preserved his identity through years of trial and triumph.

> *Your priorities in life are declared by what you say. They are proven by how you react in crisis.*

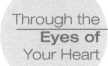

While lions' dens are out of style, many other threats pressure people who follow God. How do you show that God is your top priority even in the face of these pressures?

_____

_____

What are some ways you have been pressured to deny or restrict how you follow God? What earlier lessons in life did you rely upon to withstand the pressure?

_____

_____

_____

Have you ever paid a steep price for moral compromise? How does that mistake shape your integrity today?

_____

_____

_____

_____

A Round of Applause

> *All of you nations, come praise the LORD! Let every-one praise him. His love for us is wonderful; his faith-fulness never ends. Shout praises to the LORD!*
>
> Psalm 117 CEV

The Big Picture

In the catalog of Psalms, this four-sentence song of devotion ranks as one of the briefest. It is also among the simplest, in terms of theological presentation. Its message is so simple and so basic that it tends to be dismissed without being adequately understood.

In light of modern-day conflict and dissent, it seems unthinkable that a call to international, universal praise would be sounded, much less enjoined. People cannot even seem to get along between churches, much less nations. How can such a call to worldwide praise be attainable? Many barriers seem to prohibit this call from ever being fulfilled. The world is polytheistic. Much of the world denies the exclusive claims of Christ, and an increasing number denies the reality of God himself.

The more the modern-day plight is examined, the more desperate the psalm appears. It is almost as if the psalm resorts to defensive pleas to rally the praise. A modern eye could read this psalm with an air of desperation or even frustration.

However, to view the psalm through the jaded lens of contemporary disbelief is a serious dishonor to the truth of God's Word. Remember that this was and still is a psalm of praise written by a heart made alive by belief in God. As David does elsewhere, he creates a psalm constructed around the call to praise, the cause of praise, and the conclusion of praise. His is a simple structure, easily understood, and universally appealing. David was a witness to unending faithfulness and a recipient of divine, wonderful love. It is in this that David rallied the world in this call for praise.

This psalm was not a proclamation hoping to convince, but a conviction leading to proclamation, inviting the entire world to join. This same invitation that extends into today is even more profound because of its simplicity. In the context of seemingly unending disagreement, the Bible and nature and history harmonize to the conviction that God is praiseworthy. This psalm speaks to God's unmatched, unending faithfulness, highlighting that God has never abandoned the world he created. His deep love and high value for people are reflected in the sustaining, unwavering faithfulness he has shown in everything from food and water to air and light to luxury and comfort.

This is the Lord, as described by his nature. He indeed is worthy to be praised.

Hallelujah! Praise God in his holy house of worship, praise him under the open skies; praise him for his acts of power, praise him for his magnificent greatness; praise with a blast on the trumpet, praise by strumming soft strings; praise him with castanets and dance, praise him with banjo and flute; praise him with cymbals and a big bass drum, praise him with fiddles and mandolin. Let every living, breathing creature praise God! Hallelujah!

Psalm 150 MSG

Take a
Closer Look

Take a closer look at this easy-to-remember psalm and discover anew that God deserves praise for no other reason than because he is God. The two statements following the call to praise are not simply justifications for the call to praise; they are self-contained praises in and of themselves. The psalmist exhorts the entire world to join in the worship and adoration of God simply because he is worth it. The praise should be universal and loud and be voiced in one accord.

If you are like most people, the choices you make are based upon the benefit you receive. You choose the television programs that make you laugh or capture your imagination. You engage in hobbies or habits that make you feel good. You even choose the church you attend based on music style, which version of the Bible is used, or the length of the sermons.

However, your call to praise is not based upon what God gives back or the benefits you receive through praise. God is forever faithful, and his wonderful love is unmatched. God's faithfulness and love are not benefit enticements. They are simply truths. God deserves your worship and global praise simply because he is God.

> *Some people get angry because God put thorns on roses, while others praise him for putting roses among thorns.*
>
> Author Unknown

Your praise should not depend upon your circumstance. God deserves your praise and adoration in all times and all seasons of life simply because he is God. He is the author and sustainer of your life. As the psalmist wrote, God's love is wonderful and his faithfulness unending. These are two spiritual realities that shape your life, regardless of situation or circumstance.

Apply It
to Your Life

It can be challenging at times to praise God when life does not seem so wonderful, or when you feel as though you do not have a friend in the world. However, recalling the perspective of this brief psalm can help keep your mind-set in the right order and assist you in working through difficult times.

The children of God are expected to be the loudest voices in the universal praise of the Father. They are the ones who have experienced his wonderful love and unending faithfulness. They will lead in the chorus, not because they have received the benefit, but because they recognize most clearly who God is in his nature. God has bestowed a tremendous blessing by imparting this recognition through firsthand provision. The faithful followers of God lead the round of applause because they see God for who he is and who they are in him.

At the name of Jesus every knee will bow, in heaven and on earth and under the earth, and every tongue will confess that Jesus Christ is Lord, to the glory of God the Father.

Philippians 2:10–11 NLT

How Others
See It

The universal appeal of Psalm 117 illustrates that God's message of grace and redemption is offered to all the people of the world, and not a particular nation or race. In *Psalms,* Charles Spurgeon said:

"The nations could not be expected to join in the praise of Jehovah unless they were also partakers in the benefits which Israel enjoyed; and hence the psalm was an intimation to Israel that the grace and mercy of their God were not confined to one nation, but in happier days would be extended to all the race of man, even as Moses had prophesied."

This unbiased offering is an aspect of God's loving character, not a tool for manipulation. In a sermon based on Psalm 117, Saint Augustine said:

"You do not want to be used by anyone. You want to be loved, just for who you are, completely apart from what you may have or have not done lately. In the same way, God does not exist to be used by us, although we certainly go at God with this motive all the time, hoping to co-opt God to get us something we really want. God wants to be loved, to be enjoyed, no matter what the cost."

Zooming **In**

The Hebrew term for *nations* in Psalm 117 refers not only to the people of Israel, but also to all foreign nations. In fact, it also refers to a flight of locusts. The imagery is that a global covering of all people—all nations and people groups —would universally celebrate the nature and majesty of God.

King David is the psalmist who wrote this verse of praise. King David committed adultery and had his lover's husband murdered. Yet he was known as "a man after God's own heart" and remembered as Israel's greatest king. He faithfully praised God in all circumstances; even in his most difficult situations, he trusted in God's unending faithfulness and wonderful love.

Praise is often given as payment for a blessing. This psalm declares that praising God is appropriate for who God is, not just for what he has done.

You can apply this same principle in your other relationships. How would those you love react if you made it a habit to remind them that they are wonderful and loved just because of who they are? How would that draw you closer to each other?

_____

_____

Is it easier to worship God unconditionally by remembering that he loves you perfectly? How does your worship change when it is based on God's perfect love, instead of your imperfect performance in life?

_____

_____

How have you seen God stick with you in tough times, giving you a second or third chance? How does it make your faith stronger knowing God has not given up on you?

_____

_____

_____

Humble Pie Cures Worries

> *Humble yourselves under the mighty hand of God, that He may exalt you at the proper time, casting all your anxiety on Him, because He cares for you.*
>
> 1 Peter 5:6–7 NASB

The Big Picture

This encouraging passage is often recited to remind people that God is available to take away anxiety. A key element in the process of comfort comes through humility. This truth hints that anxiety is a subversive form of pride (thus conquered by humility).

Many years had passed since Peter was the brash man who swung the sword first before asking questions and who had denied being a follower of Jesus, despite his sincere vow to remain true. Now he was a wiser man, tested by years of service to God. His own understanding of Jesus had grown through the years, radically affecting his thoughts and conduct. His original desire to be a civic revolutionary had developed into a maturity of sacrifice toward the goal of sharing the good news of God's love for all people. He was now considered a church father, a man whose leadership was valued and trusted by Christians everywhere.

As a pastor to people in a time where it was not safe to be a Christian—admitting so could mean putting oneself at risk to be thrown to wild animals in the coliseums—he was familiar with the fear and anxiety that his people were feeling. He was no stranger to opposition and persecution, for several of his closest friends and fellow apostles had already been killed because of

take a CLOSER look

their confessed faith in Jesus of Nazareth as the Son of God. Peter knew he bore the responsibility to give the people under his care a word of hope and comfort in these troubling times when standing up as a Christian came at the risk of being immediately cut down.

To these Christians, Peter was a voice of genuine concern whose encouragement was more than empty words. He was a man who had walked in the same steps they were taking. He had, like they, faced fearful times and dangerous situations. He lived under the oppression of an unfriendly, persecuting government just as his listeners did. He understood their worries. They looked to him for insight regarding how to live well in circumstances where life itself was no guarantee.

His solution seemed almost juvenile, it was so simple. "Casting all your anxiety on Him." Yet it is the calming assurance that followed that made such instruction possible: "because He cares for you." Peter reminded his friends and fellow Christ followers that even in the heat of intense opposition, God was still there, and he still loved them. God's love for them was being expressed as open arms ready to receive all the troubles, burdens, and anxieties that they could unload.

God is unchanging. He still receives all your anxieties, if you will cast them to him. He still cares for you.

Come to me, all you who are weary and
burdened, and I will give you rest.

Matthew 11:28 NIV

A closer look at Peter's encouragement reveals insight into the sufficiency of God to be able to handle your anxieties. The verse instructs, "Humble yourselves under the mighty hand of God." Humility requires a person to admit that God is more capable than anyone to handle the problems of the world, much less the personal problems of any individual.

Anxiety is itself a subtle form of pride. When a person worries about a problem to the point of anxiety, that problem becomes bigger than God. For a person to have anxiety, he or she has to assume that God is either unaware of, unconcerned about, or unable to handle the troubling problem. Essentially, a person filled with anxiety has become self-aware to the point of idolatry. All attention, focus, and thoughts have turned inward, concentrating on the inadequacies of self rather than the mighty ability of God.

The only way any person can rise above a circumstance is by being humble before God, acknowledging his might, and relying upon his loving concern for his people. Trust God to shoulder your problems, hold you in his care, and meet your needs.

> *There is no use worrying about things over which you have no control, and if you have control, you can do something about them instead of worrying.*
>
> Stanley C. Allyn

Humility is the act of taking self-oriented thoughts and focusing them upon God. For humility to be "thinking less of oneself," the term *less* must be understood as an aspect of quantity, not quality. God does not want you to think poorly of yourself; remember, God himself said you are wonderfully made. However, God does want you

Apply It
to Your Life

to think rightly of yourself, and he does not want you to be focused on yourself, because you were never made to handle your problems on your own.

Instead of thinking about what a mess you may be in, or what a bad job you have done handling things, think instead about God. Remember the God who parted the Red Sea, who fed 5,000 people with two fish and a few loaves of bread, who walked on water, and who rose from the dead! God has shown that he thinks outside the box, and has solutions for your situation that you have not even considered. Cast your anxieties on him and invest your energy in thinking about him and trusting him. When you are humble before God, he will lift you above your troubles.

Don't worry about tomorrow. It will take care of itself.
Matthew 6:34 CEV

Worry stems from a pride-focused self-rejection, even if it originates from others. James Montgomery Boice, in *Christ's Call to Discipleship*, encourages you to focus instead on God's approval:

"The cure for our fear is knowing that we are known already—deeply and exhaustively by God himself and that he loves and receives us anyway. Humility begins by knowing that I am accepted by God. . . . If I am accepted by God, I do not need to worry about what others may think."

God unleashes blessing upon those who are able to rightly set aside worry by means of humility. In *Spiritual Warfare for Every Christian: How to Live in Victory and Retake the Land,* Dean Sherman writes:

"We have a promise from God if we humble ourselves, he will exalt us. However, if we exalt ourselves, God has promised that he will abase us. If we do not humble ourselves when we should, we are in fact exalting ourselves. It is far easier to choose humility as a way of life. A genuine humbling is always followed by an exaltation. God keeps his promises, and we should never fear humility."

Zooming **In**

The Greek word for "humble" means to assign a lower rank to another who is to be honored. The word for "might" comes from a root word depicting a hand that spans a chasm. The word for "exalt" paints a metaphor of being placed on a peak of opulence and happiness. Peter's instruction to "humble yourselves under the mighty hand of God" is an act of will that puts your problems in the hand of God, so that he can span the chasm from where you are in your trouble to the much better place where he plans for you to be.

Humility is an act of faith because it requires you to give God all your attention and to trust him to be attentive to your needs in return. By taking this step of faith, you can be free of the binding anxiety from being self-focused.

What situations cause you to be anxious? What is it about these situations that causes anxiety?

God raised the mountains and set the clouds in the sky. How is God's strength and sufficiency available to you for what troubles you?

Giving God the attention you normally reserved for yourself is an act of worship. How does this influence the way you approach typically anxious times?

Escape Route

> *No temptation has overtaken you except what is common to humanity. God is faithful and He will not allow you to be tempted beyond what you are able, but with the temptation He will also provide a way of escape, so that you are able to bear it.*
>
> 1 Corinthians 10:13 HCSB

The Big Picture

The church in Corinth during the time of the apostle Paul was a congregation that was constantly struggling. The church was established in a community that was a major transportation hub for the entire region; it was a place where several different cultures intermingled. This caused a situation where the church was constantly in turmoil because it had people who were identifying themselves as Christians, but were doing some altogether ungodly things. Paul wrote his first letter to the Corinthian church to clear up the spiritual confusion plaguing that church and to help get it refocused on honoring God with their conduct.

His letter addressed a range of subjects covering everything from marriage to social practices to litigation to orderly worship. He understood the tremendous challenges facing the Christians of Corinth as they tried to live and behave differently from their non-Christian neighbors. He knew they would face the temptations that were common in that day, affecting every aspect of life.

take a CLOSER look

The message that Paul sent to Corinth—that God was faithful and the resource to overcoming temptation—was radical to the people of this community. They lived in a culture that mixed business with religion and both with moral indiscretion. The pagan religions of Corinth were typically adopted by business trades such as stonemasons and shipping tradesmen, and drunken feasts were regularly held in pagan temples, replete with temple prostitutes, in order to please the fickle and unfaithful gods they believed to hold sway over the prosperity of their industries.

The Christian church in Corinth was at risk of becoming like their pagan counterparts. Some questionable and immoral practices were introduced as people gave in to temptations and allowed inappropriate behavior to take place. Paul stepped in to correct those errors, and to make sure that they would not continue.

He encouraged them with this passage by letting them know the temptations they faced were nothing new. He went further by combating the timeless misconception that people feel; that which tempts them is unique and embarrassing. Instead, Paul told the Christians in Corinth that all temptation is common, and that God will not give any person more than he or she can handle. Paul understood that the power in temptation is wielded when the person who is tempted feels alone and ashamed, isolated and powerless to overcome it. By reminding his friends that God is bigger than every temptation, and that every temptation is in fact manageable, he gave this struggling church a message of hope to help get their spiritual house back in order.

Whatever I have, wherever I am, I can make it through anything in the One who makes me who I am.

Philippians 4:13 MSG

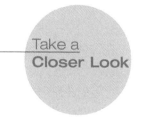

Take a Closer Look

Look closely at this passage and see that hidden within plain sight, God provides a promised escape route away from every temptation. He gives you more than the ability to withstand the temptation; he gives you a deliverance to be free from it. Endurance is a fine gift, not to be belittled. However, to be free from temptation is a greater experience than merely to be able to handle it.

Temptation can be an oppressive overlord. Knowing that certain situations, opportunities, things, or even people tempt you is like living life under house arrest. That temptation serves as a limitation on your life, restricting you from fully experiencing and exploring the grand adventure that God has planned for you. True liberty is only experienced when you are free from what tempts you, rather than merely being able to withstand its enticement. When something no longer holds sway over your thoughts, actions, and behavior, only then can you be free to do and be all that God has intended.

In fact, this passage shows that the only way to bear temptation is to escape it. Use God's escape route the next time you are tempted, and discover your life in freedom.

> *I count him braver who over-comes his desires than him who conquers his enemies; for the hardest victory is the victory over self.*
>
> Aristotle

Consider the things in your life that have you trapped in a corner of temptation. Maybe it's something you see, or something you taste, or something you touch. Think about how powerless you feel every time you are confronted by that temptation. Think about the guilt, regret, and failure you feel every time that temptation overcomes you and you give in to it.

Apply It
to Your Life

Trying to feed temptation is like throwing prey to a constantly starved, ravenous beast. It never ends. Only by realizing that God offers something better—than every temptation—can you face that beast without offering more of yourself as its food.

God's escape route may look different in each situation, but he is faithful to provide you a way that you do not have to be defeated by temptation. Maybe it is a friend who will be there for you. Perhaps God will give you a Scripture that will encourage you. Possibly he will give you a new activity or an alternate way of thinking. In reality, God gives you nothing less than himself for everything that tempts you. God promises to be better than anything that lures you because while giving in to temptations satisfies your lusts, focusing upon God satisfies your spirit.

Watch and pray so that you will not fall into temptation. The spirit is willing, but the body is weak.

Mark 14:38 NIV

Regardless of the temptation you face, God knows your limit. W. Herschel Ford, in *Sermons You Can Preach*, wrote:

"God has never promised us we will be free from temptation, but has promised a way of escape when temptation comes. Our great buildings have fire escapes. When a building is on fire, the owner does not promise to take you out bodily, but does promise a way to escape. . . . God knows our limitations and will not let Satan put too big a load on us. God is faithful in delivering all those who turn to him in time of temptation."

Bryan Chapell shares insight into the escape route in his book *Holiness by Grace: Delighting in the Joy That Is Our Strength*:

"We take advantage of the way of escape God provides by exerting every resource he gives us to fight the enemy. Sometimes he provides the way of escape by miraculous deliverance. . . . God more often allows us to escape temptation by using the means of grace always available to us: conscientiously seeking God's power and instruction through prayer, meditation on his Word, and the counsel of mature Christians [is] never passive."

Zooming **In**

Paul's encouragement to seek God's escape route is given in the context of the temptation of the Corinthian Christians to take part in the pagan rituals that were common in that region. These rituals regularly intermingled the offenses of worshiping idols, making horrible sacrifices, and then engaging in immoral activities. Paul reminded them that God had forbidden this conduct since the time of Israel's exodus under Moses. When the Israelites gave in to similar temptations, thousands met the inevitable consequence of death. Paul was not merely trying to scare Christians into doing right, but was instead warning them that giving in to temptation often comes at great expense.

Choosing God's escape route over temptation does not happen accidentally. It requires a deliberate action of turning away from the temptation and turning to God himself.

What tempts you? How would your life be different if this temptation no longer had power over you?

_____

_____

_____

_____

How do you feel when you think about the prospect of no longer being tempted by this? How does it take faith to trust that God is more fulfilling than your temptation?

_____

_____

_____

What do you need to bring into your life to make sure choosing God is always an option when you are tempted? How can a Christian friend help you overcome this temptation?

_____

_____

_____

_____

Wisdom's Own Reward

> *You know that you learn to endure by having your faith tested. But you must learn to endure everything, so that you will be completely mature and not lacking in anything. If any of you need wisdom, you should ask God, and it will be given to you. God is generous and won't correct you for asking.*
>
> James 1:3–5 CEV

The Big Picture

As the half brother of Jesus, James knew what it felt like to have doubts. He grew up with an older brother who made amazing claims, stirred up controversy, and was killed because of the words he spoke and feats he accomplished. As a young Jewish man, James was familiar with all the prophecies of God's promised Messiah. He had observed the life his sibling Jesus had led and had heard the message Jesus had preached. James needed supernatural wisdom to reconcile all of his experiences with his expectations to come to a point of belief that his half brother Jesus was, undoubtedly, the Son of God.

Now, years later, James shared encouragement with a new generation of people who shared that incredible belief. Their faith was being tested in a stress-filled culture that put people with such beliefs into coliseums to fight wild beasts, or simply tortured and executed them publicly as an example to others.

James was no stranger to these tests of faith. Now, as the leader of the Christian church in Jerusalem, he had endured persecution for years, at the hands of an assortment of civic tyrants and official persecutors. He had seen his friends murdered. He had witnessed the slaughter of peaceful people, killed simply because they, like he, believed that Jesus is God's Messiah. He had seen the Christian church pushed underground. Countless times through the years, he had seen his faith put to the test, and he now addressed a world community of Christians who were doing the same. To these friends and fellow believers, he shared the tool he used to repeatedly reconnect him with his faith that Jesus is God, to strengthen his hope, and to affirm his assurance in the certainty of his beliefs. He offered them the tool of wisdom.

In this passage, James makes the connection between wisdom and a person's ability to endure difficult times and unpleasant situations. Wisdom is the key that opens the puzzling locks of life. Wisdom seasons knowledge with understanding. It helps give a person the perspective, rationale, and comprehension to withstand events that may be otherwise unbearable. God offers wisdom freely (or abundantly) to anyone who seeks it. This key—wisdom—that unlocks life's treasures is essential, available, and affordable. All you have to do is ask for it.

Respect and obey the LORD! This is the first step to wisdom and good sense.

Psalm 111:10 CEV

If you reread this passage, you will discover that wisdom is a key to blessing, but it is also so much more. Wisdom is truly a reward unto itself. Too often, people ask for wisdom because they consider it as a vehicle to drive them to a desired result or goal. While wisdom certainly meets this need and provides this service, to use wisdom in this capacity is like using an encyclopedia for a doorstop; it can do the job, but its intended purpose is much, much greater.

God gives wisdom generously and graciously. God is eager and pleased to give you wisdom. Note that it is not anecdotal or situational. God offers wisdom that can be applied to every season and circumstance of life. In fact, wisdom is the manifestation of maturity and the proof of God's provision. When you ask for and receive God's liberal allotment of wisdom, life's challenges are bearable because you will be facing them with the treasure of insight and perspective that is far greater than what you could have possessed on your own.

> *It is a sign of conceit and immaturity to dispense with taking advice in major decisions.*
>
> J. I. Packer

Wisdom has been defined as "knowledge, applied." Wisdom is more than knowing the right thing to do, but having the strength to do it. God's wisdom is far superior to worldly wisdom because worldly wisdom is unstable, conditional, and self-ish. God's wisdom is unchanging, unconditional, and selfless.

Maturity and provision, as mentioned in this passage, are the results of receiving God's wisdom. The understanding that God offers anyone who asks is a priceless, precious gift. The ironic aspect of wisdom, though, is that it requires engagement with challenging situations for it to be necessary. James says that only by asking for wisdom can you have the insight to endure life's challenges. Conversely, only by facing life's challenges can you use the wisdom that God so freely offers.

Life, by its own nature, tests your faith. Every day you meet a challenge that requires you either to believe God or to disbelieve. Sometimes those challenges are small; sometimes they are huge. Wisdom is not simply the key to get you through those challenges. In reality, those challenges are the key by which you unlock the treasure of God's wisdom for you. When you scoop deep into the unending reserves of wisdom that God has stored, you under-stand that the wealth of God is found in applying his great perspective to every detail of life.

A wise man will hear and increase learning, and a man of understanding will attain wise counsel, to understand a proverb and an enigma, the words of the wise and their riddles.

Proverbs 1:5–6 NKJV

Wisdom is not a treasure to be discovered once in life. In fact, according to Philip Yancey and Brenda Quinn in *Meet the Bible*, wisdom is a series of keys by which you unlock the doors of life:

"Following God's guidelines for living is the first step in moving from the unwise to the wise. . . . Wisdom is found in those who take advice. . . . The choices we make in friends and how we allot our time reflect how concerned we are with gaining wisdom. . . . The words we use, the things we say, usher us deeper into or farther away from wisdom. . . . Where we place our energy and commitment represents our final key to wisdom. . . . For a person growing in wisdom, this becomes a passion that is never quenched."

For wisdom to release so many of life's locks, clearly wisdom itself is fully embodied by embracing God himself. Herbert Lockyer argues as much in his book *All the Messianic Prophecies of the Bible*:

"One of the impressive features of Solomon's notable literary production is the way he presents wisdom, not merely as a coveted attribute, but identified as a person. . . . He personified wisdom as a co-creator, as the one dwelling with God from all eternity. This wisdom is God's Son."

Zooming **In**

Several men in the Bible share the name *James*. The James who authored this book is not only the half brother of Jesus (James's most likely biological father was Joseph) and full brother of Jude, but he was also an early church leader in Jerusalem. He is mentioned in the book of Acts as being in the Upper Room praying when the Holy Spirit visited the first followers of Christ. James was martyred for following Jesus as Lord. James, who identified himself in this letter as "a bondservant of God and of the Lord Jesus Christ" (1:1 NKJV), was thrown from a high place and then beaten to death while he prayed for those who attacked him.

Wisdom is a treasure that withstands the winds of time and the waters of circumstance. Learn to value wisdom as much as the blessings that wisdom brings, and you will discover wealth that never depreciates.

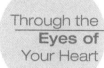

Through the
Eyes of
Your Heart

Where do you need wisdom? What are some issues you face today that trouble you, frustrate you, or even just seem to be a roadblock that you cannot move beyond?

_____

_____

Wisdom has also been described as "knowledge with a heavenly perspective." How can God's perspective change how you view your current situation? How does a fresh perspective change how you face today's challenges?

_____

_____

Lumps of coal placed under tremendous pressure form diamonds. What are some mistakes of your past (the "lumps of coal") that today, because of past pressures, are gems of wisdom that you can use for future success?

_____

_____

_____

Self-Perspective

> *I say, through the grace given to me, to everyone who is among you, not to think of himself more highly than he ought to think, but to think soberly, as God has dealt to each one a measure of faith.*
>
> Romans 12:3 NKJV

The Big Picture

In biblical times, the Romans were a proud people. They were the most powerful people in the world. Their armies had conquered the known world. To be Rome's friend was to have safety, and to be her enemy was dangerous. Romans were leaders and shapers of culture, of architecture, and of philosophical thought. They were the wealthiest citizens of the world, people who could afford to indulge in every whim and fancy.

In this regard, the message of Christianity was incredibly countercultural. In the Roman culture that claimed primacy in every aspect of life, Christianity exhorted people to be humble. In Roman life that encouraged putting one's own interests before any other concerns, Christianity encouraged individuals to do the opposite by putting everybody else's interests before one's own. It became a paradox in the "me-first" culture of Roman paganism for Christianity—in all its selflessness—to expand rapidly through the land, changing lives as well as mind-sets.

take a CLOSER look

The author of the Bible's letter to the church in Rome explained that this mental reorientation was only possible if a person would stop thinking too highly of himself or herself. The author understood the Roman culture and human nature well enough to see how most people think of themselves with an inflated, high regard. Most people think of themselves as the star of the world's drama, with everyone else playing a supporting role. He was sharing a clear message that this sort of selfish perspective was both out of place in the Christian experience and out of order with the realities of life.

The author was not advocating pessimism or hypercritical self-evaluation. He does not advocate a negative self-image. In fact, what he advocates is no self-image at all. Instead, he advocates a God-oriented opinion of yourself. If you really want to have an accurate view of the real you, God's point of view is the only one that really matters.

A self-oriented evaluation is commonly flattering, but rarely honest. We tend to minimize our shortcomings and accentuate our strengths. Sometimes, as though our perception is warped by drunkenness, we actually misidentify weaknesses as strengths. Instead of indulging in this foolish endeavor, you should instead let God introduce you to the real you. In the process, you will get to know the wonderfully made person you truly are, and you will grow closer to the wonderful God who made you.

God expects but one thing of you, and that is that
you should come out of yourself in so far as you are
a created being made and let God be God in you.

Johannes Eckhart

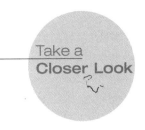

A closer look at Paul's exhortation to the Roman Christians shows that a right self-examination not only requires humility, but also is dependent upon grace, sobriety, and faith. If you are lacking any of these components, the result is an inappropriate assessment of your own identity. First, you must view your self-assessment through the perspective of God's grace, which is simply understood as God's undeserved blessing applied to your life. God's grace allows you to view yourself positively, without being unnecessarily harsh or inappropriately negative. Next, sobriety has nothing to do with alcohol but with honesty about your limitations and shortcomings. This honesty allows you to appreciate your intrinsic need for God. Finally, faith is required to complete the picture of who you truly are. Faith bridges the expanse from who you are with your limitations and shortcomings to who you are through the grace of God.

Pride oversells who you are by minimizing or falsely eliminating your flaws. Shame undermines who you are by overemphasizing the characteristics and conduct that separate you from God. Faith is the corrective lens that makes visible God's grace, which applies sufficient forgiveness to give you a healthy, whole, respectable, and accurate self-identity.

> When a man is all wrapped up in himself he makes a pretty small package.
>
> John Ruskin

Exercise your faith and examine your true self. First, take an honest look and admit what it is about you that does not please God. Maybe you cut ethical corners. Perhaps you struggle with telling the truth or gossiping. Maybe you can be unkind, unforgiving, or impatient. Whatever your flaws, just between you and God, shoot straight and acknowledge that you have your flaws.

Do not stop there, because that is only part of the picture. Now, see what the Bible says about how God sees you. You are a new creation. Your mistakes have been forgiven. Your flaws have been corrected. You are his crowning achievement in creation, and it is impossible for God to love you more or better than he does right at this very moment.

You may not feel perfect, new, forgiven, or fixed. You need faith to get from how you feel about yourself to how the Bible declares you to be. You also need faith to keep the humble understanding that God deserves all the credit for the good found in you. Maintaining this healthy self-perspective requires spiritual calisthenics that ultimately place your focus upon God and others, rather than yourself.

But for those who are self-seeking and who reject the truth and follow evil, there will be wrath and anger.

Romans 2:8 NIV

Ironically, a right view of yourself can only be attained by taking attention away from your self. John Piper said:

"In choosing faith as the measure of the new self, Paul is choosing an absolutely unique act of the new mind. What is the essence of faith? Faith is looking away from ourselves to another. Faith is total dependence on another. When faith stands in front of a mirror, the mirror becomes a window with the glory of Christ on the other side. Faith looks to Christ and enjoys him as the sum and judge of all that is true and good and right and beautiful and valuable and satisfying. . . . The essence of the new Christian mind is that we see and savor—we behold and we embrace—Jesus Christ and not ourselves as the supreme truth and supreme treasure in the universe."

Zooming **In**

To "think highly of yourself" comes from the Greek word *huperphroneo*, which contains the root meanings of "overexercising the mind." This word picture illustrates an overestimation of oneself, putting the self on equal par with God. This term has also rightly been translated as "vain arrogance."

This passage shows the spiritual opposition between pride and humility. The best way to avoid the inevitable fall that follows pride is to cling fast to the lifeline of grace, relying by faith on the fact that God is your benefactor, freely giving all the blessings you enjoy in life.

The real you is found beneath the masks you wear in front of others. Peel away the false fronts in your time alone with God so you can see yourself as God sees you.

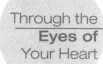

Through the
Eyes of
Your Heart

What are your least flattering qualities? What would your closest friends or spouse say to this question?

_____

_____

What factors in your life or aspects of your life have skewed your self-perspective? Have you been blinded by success, or is your vision dimmed by failures? How does honest self-evaluation challenge you to believe that God's view of you is not shaped by your performance but by your trust in him?

_____

_____

How would your life be different if you deliberately lived by faith according to what God says about you rather than by what you feel about yourself? What must change in order to live according to an unchanging, positive standard rather than a shifting, emotional feeling about yourself?

_____

_____

Copy Center

We must be sure to obey the truth we have learned already. Dear friends, pattern your lives after mine, and learn from those who follow our example.

Philippians 3:16–17 NLT

The Big Picture

The church that the apostle Paul established in Philippi was one of the earliest known churches in Europe. Paul had a deep love for this church congregation, and they felt the same toward him. The Philippians appreciated his leadership and they gave sacrificially, even when they were themselves in need, because they believed so strongly that his work of spreading the gospel must continue. The church and the apostle shared a mutual love born out of a unity in worshiping Jesus as Christ; that love sustained and blessed both groups throughout their relationship together.

In this particular letter to the Philippian church, Paul relied upon the relationship that he shared with the church to accomplish a greater purpose. He was aware of the increasing limits of his abilities. At the same time, he understood that the only way to accomplish the work God had given—to share the gospel with the world—was for the church to pursue obedience. Paul knew that these Christians must also travel to new lands and share the gospel message with new audiences around the world.

take a **CLOSER** look

The challenge lay in that call to obey God.

Obedience is never an easy sell, or even a fun topic to discuss. To choose to obey also means to choose to put personal priorities, motives, and agendas aside. When the challenge of obedience sounds, it puts the matter to the test by requiring the challenged person to either agree to obey or disagree and disobey. While Paul knew this call to obedience would be challenging to any audience, he had high expectations that the Philippians would respond properly because their pattern of living had been consistently selfless and sacrificial.

What made Paul's challenge both palatable and possible was the fact that he was encouraging them to obey what they already knew. He had spent time with them, teaching them the truth of God and the essential beliefs of the Christian faith. He had demonstrated to them the right way to think, the right way to behave, and the right way to live. He knew they could obey what was necessary because he had observed them doing so earlier. He had made certain that they possessed all the spiritual and practical tools to have a close relationship with God, experienced through obedience. He had personally given them all the tools needed to do and be all that God had planned for them.

All that remained was for them to obey.

Preach the gospel at all times. Use words if necessary.

Saint Francis of Assisi

Take a Closer Look

Read closely Paul's encouragement to his Philippian friends and see that the exhortation to obey is really a call to imitate what they already witnessed in Paul. The struggles this early church faced arose because, in effect, they had diverted from what Paul had shown them with his own life. He exhorted them to return to what they already knew because they had seen the right example in him. He was able to encourage them with this instruction because not only had he already made the initial investment in them himself, but his investment came from his personal expense.

Paul's life illustrates the principle that discipleship is reproducing in others the disciple that you yourself have come to be. He had given them the pattern to replicate. He had provided the path they could trust to follow. This was no mystic philosophy or theological system requiring reconstruction. It was simple obedience that he had himself demonstrated, showing his friends and fellow Christ followers the manner in which they, too, should conduct themselves. In the trials they would face, they only had to look at Paul's Christlike actions, and copy the model he had given.

> *Without a humble imitation of the characteristics of the Divine Author of our blessed religion, we can never hope to be . . . happy.*
>
> George Washington

The line separating following God and following another person may at times seem fine, but in fact is wide and gracious. From the beginning, Jesus determined that you should learn how to follow him not only from the instructions of the Bible, but also from the patterns established by preceding generations of godly men and women.

The Bible declares that there is nothing new under the sun. The challenges, troubles, trials, and opportunities that confront you have already been addressed in some form by those who have gone before you as they followed Christ in their own day. Look to their example and learn from it. Be encouraged by their own obedience and reproduce it. See the manner and effect of their faithful walk, and be emboldened to place your footsteps in the imprints they have left behind.

Paul has declared that the truth has already been learned. It does not need to be rediscovered, only reapplied. Whether the trailblazers teaching you are the Bible's patriarchs or merely parent figures still taking steps of faith themselves, look to them for an example and then do as they do in accordance with the unchanging Word of God.

Remember your leaders who first taught you the word of God. Think of all the good that has come from their lives, and trust the Lord as they do.

Hebrews 13:7 NLT

Imitation of this discipline is possible when the object of the effort is Jesus, rather than the mentor. Joni Eareckson Tada wrote in *More Precious Than Silver*:

"Paul is not asking us to imitate his righteousness, for there is only one that is holy, and he is the Lord. Paul is asking us to imitate the choices he makes, to model his discernments and response to certain people and situations. . . . We imitate the methods and manners of the Christians who serve as our examples. The Christlikeness, the holiness and righteousness will then be added."

For the Christian to step forward and encourage others to imitate her as she imitates Christ requires a marathoner's mentality, according to Randal Roberts, who wrote in his book *Lessons in Leadership*:

"A marathoner develops a life characterized by recognizing the need for—and the welcoming of—discipline. He wants to waste no time heading toward a direction that is not toward the finish. . . . Aspiring to Christian leadership is a wonderful thing—being called to it even more so. Remember, it is a call to a race . . . a marathon that will test every fiber in your being."

Zooming **In**

Christians first earned their name from nonbelievers in the town of Antioch, who mocked the disciples of Jesus by calling them "little Christs" for the manner in which they imitated their Messiah in sacrificial service and devoted love to one another and others.

Imitation has long been a tradition in rabbinical schools, where respected rabbis are sought out by pupils so they can sit under the rabbi's teaching and learn to imitate his conduct and teachings, reproducing each for subsequent generations.

Someone once said that you make the type of disciple that you are yourself. This should encourage as well as compel you to be a good example to those looking at you as their model.

Who has made a significant impression on you in your life? What was it about those people that caused you to want to be like them?

_____

_____

_____

Who is looking up to you? What are you telling them about Jesus by the way you speak and act?

_____

_____

_____

How does it make you feel to know that somebody may be watching you to learn more about God? What do you need to change to make sure that you are giving them a reliable model to imitate themselves?

_____

_____

_____

Water You Are Waiting For

Joshua said, *"By this you shall know that the living God is among you. . . . It shall come about when the soles of the feet of the priests who carry the ark of the LORD, the Lord of all the earth, rest in the waters of the Jordan, the waters of the Jordan will be cut off, and the waters which are flowing down from above will stand in one heap."*

Joshua 3:10, 13 NASB

**The
Big Picture**

The Israelites—God's people—had wandered in the desert for forty long years. Four decades had passed since they had been delivered from the perils of the oncoming chariots of Pharaoh. All the adults who led the families of that day had died. Their leader Moses had also recently died, and they now followed the brave man named Joshua, once the chief spy and right-hand man of Moses.

At Moses' death, Joshua stood before the multitude of his countrymen and told them the ambitious plan given to him by God. It was the plan that they would follow. They would cross the mighty, raging waters of the Jordan River and claim possession of the land that had been promised to them by God.

This task was no small undertaking. They must consider the powerful enemies who already occupied the land and would surely be waiting for them in battle. Years earlier, Israel had surveyed the land and learned of their giant foes. Yet they believed that God was leading them, so they bravely made

take a CLOSER look

their plans to ford the Jordan and take over their lands. Little did they know that while the Israelites planned, God had filled the soldiers of Jericho with dread at the thought of the Israelite invasion. They had heard the legends of the might of the Israeli people whose God went before them. No foe had ever opposed them and survived. God's victory over Egypt's pharaoh forty years earlier still resounded through the lands. Now God was again going before them, winning the battle before the conflict ever started.

First, though, there was the matter of crossing the Jordan. The banks of the river were steep, and the waters rushed violently. Common sense and logic said that any person who stepped over the edge would certainly die, and likely never be seen again. As row after row of the nation of Israel approached the bank, conversations of fear, doubt, or even dismay were swallowed by the loud roar of churning water. Standing on the shores would not manifest the miracle of God. The command that had been given to the entire camp was that their spiritual leaders must first step into the waters before their military leaders could step onto the battlefield. Once again, God's children were required to take a literal step of faith.

Faith is not belief. Belief is passive. Faith is active.

Edith Hamilton

Look over the banks of the raging Jordan River to see that this step of faith was not merely the first stride toward the promised land; it was also the realization that nothing and nobody could stop God's plan for his people. After forty years of wandering and the death of Moses, no quick-flowing river was going to overcome what God had prepared for Israel.

It is no coincidence or accident that God's people once again found themselves on the water's edge facing a situation where they had to trust God to provide the path to take them where he had promised. Deliverance through the Red Sea's waters brought them safely from initial harm, then they wandered aimlessly in their own efforts for the next four decades. Now they had to decide again to trust God in spite of all physical evidence in order to see the fulfillment of what he pledged to give them.

Remember, too, that this decision was one requiring spiritual courage more than military fortitude or personal bravery. There would be no testing the waters with a big toe. Either they were all in or they were all out. To step forward required a full commitment, no matter the result. They determined to trust God at all costs.

Remember: With fulfillment comes responsibility.

Bill Cosby

Today you might find yourself on a proverbial shore facing a similar situation. On the other side of the obstacle you face, you can see the promised blessing that God has offered. Yet you cannot get there on your own, and the raging waters of the uproar have consumed your attention.

God has said from the beginning to trust him. He has promised that he will give you safe travel through this calamity, not around it. There is nothing logical or natural about this claim. Everything that you can see or hear threatens otherwise, yet the promise remains.

You can look over your shoulder and remember how God has delivered you in the past. Take courage and find comfort in the reality that he does not change. The promises that God has made to you have not expired over time or become invalid because of inconsistencies on your part. You cannot test the waters, for no faith is required for a test that bears no results. Do not be content to soak your toe when God bids you to step knee-deep by faith, only to see the waters stand in a heap before your foot settles safely—and dryly—on the river's floor.

The Lord's people may suffer a lot, but he will always bring them safely through.

Psalm 34:19 CEV

Your opportunity to take a step of faith can be the greatest experience you have ever faced, but you will never see it until you take the actual step. John Ortberg, in his Bible study *Stepping Out in Faith,* wrote:

"The truth is, everybody faces the Jordan many times in his or her life. Everybody faces barriers. If we are not careful, these experiences can keep us from leading the type life God wants. We can be like the first generation in the desert who refused to cross the Jordan and died in the desert. Or we can take that first step into the Jordan, watch the waters part, and enter into God's adventure."

Tony Evans added in *Time to Get Serious*:

"Faith is asking you to take a risk. You are being asked to step out there on stuff you do not know and have not seen simply because someone told you to do it. . . . You do not need a lot of faith. . . . The issue of faith is not the amount of your faith, but the object of your faith."

Zooming **In**

The Jordan River originates from three springs around the base of Mount Hermon in Southwest Asia. It is the water source for the Sea of Galilee as well as the Dead Sea. Once spilling into the Dead Sea, its waters have no source for outflow and dehydrate there, far below sea level.

The Jordan River is mentioned several times in Scripture. It is where Jacob wrestled with God, where many Ephraimites were slain by Jephthah, where Gideon waited to attack the Midianites, where Solomon set up industry, where Elijah and Elisha performed miracles, and where John baptized Jesus of Nazareth.

> *Stepping out in faith is a bold action of courageous obedience to God. It may not always make sense, but God blesses you when you trust him.*

Through the
Eyes of
Your Heart

What faith steps have you taken in the past? How did God provide for you in the face of risk?

_____

_____

_____

What faith step is in your immediate future? What do you risk by not taking the step?

_____

_____

_____

How will other people around you be impacted if they witness you take a step of faith? What will your actions show them about God?

_____

_____

_____

_____

If the Shoe Fits

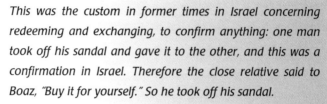

This was the custom in former times in Israel concerning redeeming and exchanging, to confirm anything: one man took off his sandal and gave it to the other, and this was a confirmation in Israel. Therefore the close relative said to Boaz, "Buy it for yourself." So he took off his sandal.

Ruth 4:7–8 NKJV

The Big Picture

As a Moabite widow, Ruth had to decide whether to stay or go. After the death of her husband, his dad, and his brother, she was one of three women suddenly with nothing. Her mother-in-law, Naomi, was returning to Israel, where a long famine had ended. She could accompany Naomi to Israel, and together they could try to build a meager life in poverty, or she could stay in Moab and return to her birth family.

Ruth could not go back to the life of her youth. She had fallen in love not only with her husband, but also with his family and his God. She no longer identified herself as a Moabite, but as a daughter to Naomi and a follower of her God, the God of Israel.

When Ruth and Naomi returned to Israel at the time of the barley harvest, Ruth immediately went to work providing for them. Taking advantage of the law that allowed the poor to collect any grain that landowners let fall to the ground in their harvesting, Ruth set to collect food for herself and Naomi. In doing so, she caught the attention of Boaz, the property's owner. He recognized her as the widow of his distant kin and showed her kindness by instructing his crop harvesters to leave extra grain for her to gather.

Naomi deserves credit as a shrewd woman with an eye for matchmaking. She saw more than generosity in Boaz's gift. She saw affection and hope in his actions. Naomi knew of the laws that allowed a distant relative to assume the debts and properties of a widow, and she led Ruth to place herself at Boaz's feet to see if he would accept the voluntary debt in the name of love.

Naomi judged Boaz correctly. He was willing to assume the family responsibility of Ruth's household. There was still one hurdle remaining. A kinsman, of closer relationship than Boaz, had the legal right of first claim. When the nearer kinsman realized that buying the property also required him to marry a widow, he gave up his rights because it threatened his own inheritance. Ceremonially, the nearer kinsman removed his sandal and placed it on the table, sealing that Boaz would meet their needs instead. He would marry Ruth and welcome her household into his own. God met their needs using the law, fulfilled by an act of sacrificial love.

There is no redemption from hell.

Pope John Paul II

As you take another look at the timeless story of Ruth, see beyond the classic lessons of fidelity and blessing and discover that Boaz is more than a generous and loving groom. He is also a picture of Jesus himself and a model of how Christ is Kinsman Redeemer to people today.

Boaz, too, was such a man, extending himself beyond what the law required, while fulfilling the high standards of the law. His actions were uncommon, due to the personal expense required in assuming the widows into his own family. Yet, motivated by his love for Ruth, Boaz acted faithfully and claimed them unto himself.

Generations later, Jesus would complete the picture of Kinsman Redeemer by dying on a cross and in effect paying the price for all people in need, claiming them unto himself. Just as the law required Boaz to assume the debt of the widows, so, too, does the law require Jesus to assume the debt for your sin. That debt is death, and when Jesus went to the cross, he paid that debt. Because that debt is paid, you are free to live! Motivated by love for you, Jesus paid the price so that you could enjoy the privileges that are rightfully his.

I do not pray for success, I ask for faithfulness.

Mother Teresa of Calcutta

Everybody is owned. No person is free unto herself. Even if she thinks that no one owns her (including God), her self owns her. If this is the case, there is no crueler overseer than self, subjected to the enslavement of her own whims, passions, or passing interests or indulgences.

However, if you believe that Jesus is Lord, your very belief is the receipt proving he has purchased you as your Kinsman Redeemer. This means that he owns you and has rights over you. This is what it means to call Jesus "Lord."

By identifying with Jesus through faith in him as Lord, you now can enjoy the blessings he offers as Lord. You no longer have to be satisfied with the proverbial table scraps and leftover blessings as a needy debtor. By rights, you can claim God's very best.

Before you start running up charges on the credit card, understand that God's blessings are spiritual much more than material. As the Kinsman Redeemer, Jesus provides eternal peace and hope, the blessed assurance of heaven. He offers comfort, rest, and satisfaction amid all life's circumstances. To spend this inexhaustible capital, though, you must agree to be identified in him, accepting his benevolence. To do so is to agree that his gracious lordship is superior to your own merciless self-enslavement.

God, who got you started in this spiritual adventure, shares with us the life of his Son and our Master Jesus. He will never give up on you. Never forget that.

1 Corinthians 1:9 MSG

Because of the example shown through Boaz, you can identify with Jesus as both Kinsman and Redeemer. Jeff Doles wrote in *Healing Scriptures and Prayers*:

"There is an indication of intimacy with this name, for he is identified as our redeemer. . . . More specifically, he is our Kinsman Redeemer, that is, one who acts on the behalf of his next of kin to ransom, redeem, or deliver. . . . Jesus is the Lord of Hosts, the Kinsman Redeemer who defends and delivers us in every situation."

Don Aycock and Mark Sutton added in *Still God's Man*:

"Jesus Christ is our 'kinsman redeemer.' The Bible tells us that Jesus walked like us and talked like us while on the earth. That is because he is related to us. Jesus called himself the Son of Man many times. But Jesus is powerful enough that he could redeem you and me from the slave block of sin. The great news is that he is willing to do that, going to the cross so that we may have freedom from Satan and new life in Christ."

Zooming **In**

The transaction where Boaz claimed Ruth as his own took place at the city gate, a popular setting for many events in the Bible. It was where commerce took place, where civic leaders could be seen, where criminal punishment was issued, where proclamations were made, and even where gossip was spread.

As widows living in the times of the judges, where "people did what was right in their own eyes," Ruth and Naomi had no advocates and were at high risk of being taken advantage of in their culture. The news of the drought's end in Jerusalem was indeed good news for the women, because the laws of Israel were more generous to impoverished widows.

It is important to view Jesus as both Kinsman and Redeemer. By doing so, you can understand how he fulfills the law with his love for you to offer the gifts of eternity.

Have you ever inherited anything? How did it make you feel to know that your relative thought specifically about you in giving you a gift?

_____

_____

_____

Have you ever had a relative get you out of a tough situation, even making a sacrifice to do so? How did his or her actions show love for you?

_____

_____

_____

As Redeemer, God paid the price for your soul so that you could inherit heaven. How does being identified as a child of God change how you live your life?

_____

_____

_____

Disgraced in Death

Saul said to his armor-bearer, "Draw your sword and run me through, or these uncircumcised fellows will come and run me through and abuse me." But his armor-bearer was terrified and would not do it; so Saul took his own sword and fell on it. When the armor-bearer saw that Saul was dead, he too fell on his sword and died with him. So Saul and his three sons and his armor-bearer and all his men died together that same day.

1 Samuel 31:4–6 NIV

The Big Picture

Saul is perhaps history's greatest example of a man who had it all, only to foolishly lose everything. By biblical account, he was handsome, strong, and popular. When he was named king of Israel, the people cheered and celebrated. In assuming Israel's throne, he had been handed more wealth, power, and influence than he ever imagined possible as a child of the nation's least important tribe.

As Saul's reign stretched into its fourth decade, he began to rely upon himself rather than upon God. He began to make moral compromises, and then to even disobey the instructions of God in how he led as a military ruler. Eventually, the prophet Samuel told Saul that God would no longer show favor to him as king.

This news was devastating to Saul, but rather than leading him to admit the error of having a pride-filled, ego-driven heart, he continued down the path of self-sufficiency. Lies, distrust, and conniving became the characteris-

take a CLOSER look

tics by which King Saul was known. Saul became bitter, envious, and murderous, plotting to kill the young warrior named David, simply because David had slain the mighty giant Goliath and was now more popular than the king himself.

Saul relentlessly pursued David, desperate to kill the young man he perceived to be a threat to his throne. Twice in his pursuits, he actually found himself unwittingly at the mercy of David. Both times, David's kindness not only preserved Saul's corrupted life, but highlighted the wretchedness of the king's condition by comparison to David's virtue.

As people tend to do when suffocating in their own sins, Saul separated himself further from God. Rather than consulting the Lord about his future, he sought insight from a witch. Saul had taken all the blessings God had given and squandered them. And then he went into battle.

Without the support of his God, with no friends, and only his loyal sons to support him, Saul found himself in a battle against his enemies and was quickly overmatched. He could not even convince his armor-bearer to mercifully kill him to protect him from torturous abuse. In a final act of ignobility, he fell on his own sword, a pitiful conclusion to a life that had begun with such promise.

Do not judge, or you too will be judged.
Matthew 7:1 NIV

Take a
Closer Look

In the historical account of the ascent of King David, it would be tempting to pass quickly by the ignominious end of King Saul's life. However, pausing here for a closer look at Saul's death shows how the Lord faithfully honors those who honor him and dishonors those who dishonor him.

Few people in the annals of history could brag of the potential that accompanied Saul. Possessing every earthly measure of popularity, power, and prestige, Saul had everything necessary to be remembered as one of history's great kings. Unfortunately, he was a man of little character, and it was not long before he began to compromise himself morally, ethically, and spiritually. To make matters worse, Saul actually put himself in opposition to God. He sought ungodly solutions to his challenges by seeking counsel from witches. He attempted to murder David, ignoring the favor God placed on the young man's life.

The utter disregard that Saul demonstrated for the plan of God established the path to the king's embarrassing death. The sons he cherished violently perished. The troops he commanded soon left him abandoned. Even the armor-bearer who first aided him ultimately disobeyed him. In disgrace, Saul fell on his own sword and would forever be remembered as the conquered coward who had it all and foolishly let it slip through his greedy fingers.

> *The follies of youth become the vices of manhood and the disgrace of old age.*
>
> Author Unknown

Every person should learn two lessons from the mistakes of King Saul. First, trust God to perfectly execute justice. God is patient and long-suffering, but he is just and he will not be mocked. It might break your heart to see injustice. It might infuriate you to witness oppression. It might terrify you to be subject to another's mercilessness. Rest assured, no

evil conduct goes unnoticed, and God will issue judgment upon each and every malicious deed, word, and motive.

This same promise of justice that may encourage you concerning the conduct of others should compel you toward gentleness and peaceful conduct in your own life. God is no fear-inducing taskmaster. However, the reality of God's faithful and appropriate judgment should rightfully produce a desire for a right response in you. Determine to see God's smiling face rather than to witness his stern hand. Honor God with your words, with your deeds, and with your motives. Give him the credit for your accomplishments, and take responsibility for your errors. Live in such a way that you never have to pay the price of disgrace for your disobedience.

Pride comes before destruction, and an arrogant spirit before a fall.

Proverbs 16:18 HCSB

Desperate for justice, no one need look any further than the cross upon which Jesus died to see God's utter intolerance toward evil. Dietrich Bonhoeffer wrote in *A Testament to Freedom*:

"Where is God's judgment on the godless of this earth? Not in invisible misfortune, failure or disgrace in the eyes of this world, but solely on the cross of Jesus Christ. Is not that enough for us? Do not we see all the enemies of God fallen and condemned in this cross of Christ? What is the good of all our anxiety that wants to see even more of this judgment of God? For that reason, when we begin to doubt God's judgment on earth, let us look to the cross of Christ—here is judgment, here is a free pardon. Today the crucified One in this love is still concealing from us what we will see one day in the last judgment, the salvation of the just and the damnation of the godless."

Zooming **In**

Saul's determination to murder David would have had profound effects on his own family. By this time, David had married Saul's daughter Michal, and Saul's son Jonathan was the young shepherd's best friend.

Saul had sought counsel from the Witch of Endor, ironically after he had banished all the witches and sorcerers from the land. His trusted prophet Samuel had died, and God had not spoken to King Saul. In his fear, he departed from the godly instruction Samuel had given, as well as from the pledge he had himself made, and sought the witch's ungodly advice.

God alone judges fairly. Trust him to make good decisions, and release the judgment of others to him.

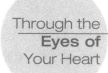

Through the
Eyes of
Your Heart

What is the difference between having discernment and being judgmental? How have you seen the difference in how you view others, or in how others view you?

_____

_____

_____

How have you seen God honor you as you have honored him? How have you seen God dishonor those who have dishonored him?

_____

_____

_____

_____

How can trusting in God's faithful judgment free you to have healthier relationships?

_____

_____

_____

_____

Battle Plan

When the Philistines heard that they had anointed David king over Israel, all the Philistines went up to seek out David; and when David heard of it, he went down to the stronghold. Now the Philistines came and spread themselves out in the valley of Rephaim. Then David inquired of the LORD, saying, "Shall I go up against the Philistines? Will You give them into my hand?"

2 Samuel 5:17–19 NASB

The Big Picture

Throughout his life, King David was known as a mighty warrior. His courage knew no limits, and fear held no sway over him. He pushed his men into battle and seemed to win virtually every conflict, regardless of the number, size, or strength of the enemy. He won when he was undermanned, underequipped, and out-maneuvered. If he met an enemy on the battlefield, David emerged victorious, almost without exception.

The youngest son of a family of shepherds, David was an unlikely warrior. He did not grow up with military training. He did not grow up learning strategy, philosophy, or battle plans. Rather, he spent his youth out in the pastures, protecting his family's flock from predators. He chased away hungry lions and rescued imperiled lambs. When other boys practiced with swords and shields, David practiced throwing smooth stones until he could hit a target with deadly accuracy. This unlikely leader had been conditioned his entire life for the demands of warfare, and when those demands pressed David into service, he responded according to his lifetime of unconventional preparation.

After years of avoiding the murderous hand of his predecessor, King Saul, David had himself become king. He would reign for forty years and establish a throne known for its military power, incredible wealth, and pursuit of God. Such a reign invited the never-ending assault of enemies.

David's foremost foes were the Philistines, enemies he had made himself for a lifetime when he had killed the mighty Goliath many years earlier. Now, after countless more exploits and victories, David was both feared and reviled by these foes. When they became aware that he had become king, they made killing him a top priority, regardless of his skills and reputation. They waited as patiently as possible as David established himself in Jerusalem, preparing themselves for the inevitable war that would come in the hopes that they might kill David and conquer the city for themselves.

David soon caught word of the Philistine military buildup, and he once again prepared himself for war. He left the comforts of his family and prepared to encounter his enemy. Yet, before he strapped on his armor and sharpened his steel, he did something that might seem altogether out of place.

He paused and asked God if this was a battle the Lord had ever intended for the king of Israel to fight.

You will not go out in haste, nor will you go as fugitives; for the LORD will go before you, and the God of Israel will be your rear guard.

Isaiah 52:12 NASB

**Take a
Closer Look**

King David was known as a warring, victorious king. Foe after foe fell beneath the strength of his mighty army. Reading the details of the accounts of his battle plans, such as found in this passage, you learn that David made a habit of being one step behind God when facing mighty strongholds.

The Philistines were longtime foes to Israel, repeatedly at war trying to overtake their land. The Philistines were known and feared for their size and for their ferocity. David had dealt with them in the past and had defeated them when he slew their fiercest warrior, Goliath. Accordingly, they wanted to kill David and were ready to do whatever was necessary to accomplish this goal.

It would be understandable for David to rush headlong into battle against the Philistines, particularly because he had defeated them in the past. He could have presumed that God was on his side and would aid him in his war. To his credit, though, David did not assume on past victories and determined to submit to the leading of God. He sought to affirm his position in accordance with God and in deference to God. He recognized that the most important step in a winning battle plan is to first go before God and seek his favor.

> *If we fight the Lord's battles merely by duplicating the way the world does its work, we are like little boys playing with wooden swords pretending they are in the battle while their big brothers are away in some distant bloody land.*
>
> Francis Schaeffer

You will find yourself in a stronghold from time to time, preparing to face an enemy and planning how to come out victorious. Your foe may be another person, someone who is trying to wrong you or to prosper unfairly at your expense. Maybe, though, your foe is a circumstance or a situation that must be overcome or persevered through. Learn from David's example and seek God before you advance into battle.

There are times when you will not be able to account for the aggressive actions of others. Perhaps they are angry because God has shown you favor, or maybe they just want what God has given to you. In David's situation, it was land and a kingdom. In yours, it may be a job, or a title, or a promotion, or a possession. Regardless, do not rush in to fight a battle before the time is right.

Like David, you may have claimed victory over this adversary in a prior conflict. You might have cause to be bold. Yet be wise and do not allow your bold behavior to give way to brash conduct. Before you enter into conflict of any kind, take the time to make sure you, too, are acting in accordance with God and in deference to God. Recognize that God is the one who will fight and win your battles. Seek his favor and trust him for the outcome.

There is no wisdom, no insight, no plan that can succeed against the LORD. The horse is made ready for the day of battle, but victory rests with the LORD.

Proverbs 21:30–31 NIV

David made a regular habit of talking with God before engaging his enemy. Jim Cymbala, in his book *Fresh Faith*, writes of another such encounter where the same principles speak to believers today:

"David was 'a man after God's own heart' because he humbly asked God's direction for his daily life. He knew that if he did not have the umbrella of God's supply, he had no business tangling with the Philistines. . . . He asked for God's plan, and in this case, God said yes—go ahead. Even then, David came back a second time. . . . The answer again was yes. . . . David triumphed over the Philistines . . . and all of this happened because he inquired upon the Lord."

Marilyn Hontz writes in *Listening for God* that the same practice David undertook to hear from the Lord is a discipline you, too, can develop:

"Strive to grow in your intent to be attentive to the Holy Spirit. . . . Stopping to hear God's voice does not come naturally at first—or all the time—for anyone. . . . Invite God to interrupt you. . . . After the Holy Spirit has your attention, then be available. Finally, listening comes down to this: obedience. . . . Learn to listen for God. If you do, you are in for an incredible journey."

Zooming **In**

Despite being a brave, victorious warrior, David also had times early in his life when he was fearful and hid to protect his life from murderous King Saul. It was in these times of hiding that David discovered characteristics of God as a mighty fortress, a strong shield, and a solid rock.

In earlier conflicts with King Saul, David had sent out advance scouts to warn him of the situation and to provide a preliminary view of the challenge that faced him. These scouts gave him an accurate understanding of what the situation presented, and how best to handle it. David ultimately realized that no scout could improve upon the preliminary counsel of God.

Spending time with God before you face conflict will not only help you in the heat of the moment, but it will likely help you avoid many unnecessary fights altogether.

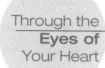

Through the
Eyes of
Your Heart

Have you ever rushed into a conflict over a misunderstanding? How would you have handled the situation differently with more forethought?

When you have found yourself in conflict, how did God show you different solutions to your problem? How did these alternate solutions prove to be better than your original plans?

What does it mean to you for God to fight your battles? How do you see your role if God is doing your fighting for you?

Seasonal Temptations

Then Jesus was led up by the Spirit into the wilderness to be tempted by the Devil. And after He had fasted 40 days and 40 nights, He was hungry. . . . Then the Devil left Him, and immediately angels came and began to serve Him.

Matthew 4:1–2, 11 HCSB

The Big Picture

At the onset of the earthly ministry of Jesus of Nazareth, he spent forty days and nights fasting in the desert. The Bible records this time as one of testing and temptation where the Messiah was confronted and repeatedly challenged by Satan.

The Bible tells readers that Jesus was filled with the Holy Spirit and did not eat this entire time. He was spiritually strong but physically weak. Perhaps, then, it is no surprise that Satan first attempted to challenge Jesus by using the gnawing hunger in the Messiah's belly. He tempted Jesus to turn stones into bread.

This feeble attempt was quickly thwarted, and the adversary increased the stakes. He tempted Jesus on the grounds of whether or not Jesus was indeed the Son of God, daring him to throw himself down from the temple and be rescued by an army of angels. Surely, Satan reasoned, if the crowd of people witnessed such a miracle, they would fall to their faces and worship Jesus.

Jesus, though, saw through Satan's ploy and again denied the devil. In a third effort of escalating proportions, Satan then offered Jesus all that was temporarily his . . . all the kingdoms of the world. For the third time, Jesus rebutted the devil and Satan departed, utterly defeated in his attempts to derail the work of Jesus before it began.

In this account, Jesus thrice denied Satan from each real temptation using the Word of God as his weapon of defense. Satan's temptations were real. Jesus was hungry and desired to eat. Jesus was the Son of God, and it was tempting to simply win the crowd's devotion with an unplanned act of drama. Jesus was Lord of all, yet Satan's offer would have meant the Cross was unnecessary. However, the price tag of each offer was unreasonable, and God had already accounted for the means necessary to overcome these tempting offers.

In relying upon the Word of God as his defense, Jesus not only withstood the enemy, but provided a reliable model for anyone facing temptation who followed. Jesus demonstrated the sufficiency of God's Word to withstand any enticement. He showed that the promises of God are more reliable than anything that tempts the eye, the heart, and even the belly. He also revealed that God's promises precede worldly temptations and can be trusted long after the temptations pass away in futility.

Give not place to Satan, no, not an inch in his first motions; he that is a beggar, and a modest one without doors, will command the house if let in.

William Gurnall

**Take a
Closer Look**

You may be familiar with the biblical account of Satan's early attempt to derail the mission of Jesus through the desert temptation. Take a closer look at the story. Not only did Satan fail, but when he failed, he was forced to depart from the Lord. When Satan's futile efforts to tempt Jesus proved unfruitful, it was impossible for Satan to remain in the presence of Jesus.

The temptations that Satan offered were real and alluring. Apart from tempting, though, Satan has no initial power. He only gains additional power when he is successful in the initial temptation. Once he leads someone to fulfill a temptation, then Satan can employ guilt, fear, intimidation, and threats.

Satan demonstrates that his tactics, while historically effective, are limited. He arrives on the scene with a skillful mix of half-truths and full deceptions. When Jesus denied Satan's advances, the adversary had no other option than to flee from the holy presence of the Christ. The Word of God stops temptation, silences the enemy, and sends him fleeing.

> *Sin is not an unfortunate slip or a regrettable act; it is a posture of defiance against a holy God.*
>
> Max Lucado

The same tactics Jesus used to send away the enemy will work in your life when you face temptations. It does not matter if it is as small as the temptation to overeat, or as serious as the temptation to commit adultery, or as eternally significant as the temptation to oppose God. In the face of every enticement, God has provided a remedy

in his Word to correct you and encourage you. He has provided you with an antidote to Satan's poisonous lies, and with the Bible, you have power over this enemy.

Realize that Satan is behind every temptation. Do not minimize him by imagining him with tiny horns and a pitchfork as he whispers thoughts in your ears. Do not deny his reality by attributing the temptation to something other than what it is. Rather, acknowledge the effort behind what you cannot see and combat that effort with the truth of God's Word.

Satan may persist for a while in trying to distract you, to derail you, or even to destroy you. Your sure response in each circumstance is to trust wholly upon biblical truth to reveal the falsehoods you will face. Ultimately, not only will you overcome the temptations, but you will overcome the tempter.

For whatever is born of God overcomes the world; and this is the victory that has overcome the world—our faith. Who is the one who overcomes the world, but he who believes that Jesus is the Son of God?

1 John 5:4–5 NASB

How Others See It

Just as Jesus relied upon the Word of God for his ability to rebut Satan, believers can rely upon Jesus as "the Living Word" to do so today. R. T. France explains Christ's sufficiency for this task in *Jesus the Radical*:

"So the 'temptation' in fact proved an occasion for a further and more down-to-earth grasp of what Jesus' mission was going to involve. To be Messiah and Son of God was not going to be a formula for spectacular success, but for unquestioning trust and obedience, even when his Father's purpose led to a style of life and death that few Jews would have expected of the 'son of David.'"

Tom Elliff writes in *Passion for Prayer*:

"When we come against the Adversary in the name of Jesus, because we are his blood-bought children, and when we resist him by employing the actual Word of God, the promises of Scripture, we will find it far easier to deal with temptation by overcoming the Tempter. It is important for a believer to fill his heart with the Word of God. Doing so is the equivalent of stocking your spiritual ammunition belt with artillery, deadly in its effect, to throw against Satan as he and his emissaries throw temptation at you."

Zooming In

The name Satan is one of more than thirty biblical titles for the adversary of God, the fallen angel Lucifer. Many of these names are actually descriptions of his motives and conduct against the lives of humans. The works of Satan embodied in his titles include tempting, deception, stealing, intimidating, lying, and even murdering. He is called antichrist, Abbadon, Beelzebub, Apollyon, Belial, and devil. He was created as an angel of light but is now the angel of the bottomless pit. He is the Father of Lies and the Son of Perdition. He is pictured as a dragon, a roaring lion, and a serpent. He is identified as a prince or ruler over the earth and as a power or authority over darkness. None of the names of Satan are friendly or positive, and all indicate the hatred he has for people as God's finest creation and accordingly the object of his wrath.

The temptation you face may seem more "real world" than turning stones into bread. However, the resource for overcoming your enticement is the same as it was for Jesus, and if you use it, the liberating result will be the same, as well.

Through the
Eyes of
Your Heart

Have you ever found yourself more tempted than normal, where you were particularly vulnerable? What were the circumstances that opened you to the temptation?

How has God's truth helped you overcome temptation in the past? What passages from the Bible stand out to refute the temptations you have faced?

When you overcome temptation, the enemy departs from you for a time. How does it make you feel to know that trusting God to overcome temptation sends away both the pitfall-causing potential and the one who digs the pit as a trap for you?

Hair-Razing Situation

Delilah lulled Samson to sleep with his head in her lap, and she called in a man to shave off his hair, making his capture certain. And his strength left him.

Judges 16:19 NLT

The Big Picture

If ever there was a biblical personality tailor-made for a Hollywood film, it would be Samson. A man with unmatched strength, beguiling wit, and a hair-trigger temper. He struck fear into his family and his foes alike because they never knew what would set him off, and they were terrified at the prospect of the havoc he would wreak if the mood possessed him.

Their dread was well justified. His methods were destructive and nothing was safe in the path of his fury. He burned to the ground the fields of his enemies and single-handedly killed a multitude of them in murderous revenge. This brash man was soon widely known for his exploits and became a ruling judge over Israel for twenty years.

To call Samson passionate would be an understatement. When he wanted an enemy Philistine woman for his wife, nobody could change his mind, not even his parents. Later, when he wanted to visit a prostitute in the middle of his enemy's land, he did so without regard, even carrying away their city gate

take a CLOSER look

to taunt them for their inability to thwart him. When he set his mind to pursue the wild-hearted Delilah, he ignored the risks and went after her. Through her, Samson's enemies discovered the judge's weaknesses and connived with Delilah to destroy their mighty foe.

The Philistines quickly arranged a conspiracy with Delilah. They would use her to lull Samson into rest, and they would attack. Two times, she led him to the brink of capture, only to see him quickly overcome his attackers. Led by his passions instead of by his intellect, he ultimately shared that his strength was found in his hair, never cut as part of the Nazirite vow that his mother made at his birth. Finally, they had what they needed to overthrow their foe. What they could not gain from him in battle or take by force, they now could steal by manipulation and coercion. They had to resort to trickery and deception because they had no hope of defeating him on any fair, straightforward terms.

Delilah did succeed in calming her raging lover into a vulnerable sleep. His enemies rushed in while he slept upon her lap; they shaved his head, robbing him of his strength. His might left him, and he was powerless to combat or resist the vengeful plans of his Philistine enemies who would finally themselves rest comfortably because they had vanquished the terrifying Israelite judge Samson.

Our power is not so much in us as through us.
Harry Emerson Fosdick

A closer look at the sad defeat of Samson shows that his defeat was the result of more than a bad haircut—it was the result of a long wayward walk down a path of immorality. All along the way, he dishonored his vows to follow God as a Nazirite.

When Samson was born, his mother had vowed to consecrate him for the Nazirite priesthood. She was setting him apart as an act of worship, so that he might live for God. She never cut his hair, and she led him to live a life of moral purity.

As he entered adulthood, though, Samson's impetuousness gave way to indulgence. He compromised his moral standards and began pursuing relationships with immoral, ungodly women. He repeatedly gave in to his passions and his furies, often with dramatic and deadly consequences.

When Samson finally succumbed to Delilah, it was no accident or real surprise. Samson had worked with determination to be brought down by his own weaknesses. The only real surprise was that he withstood his enemies' advances as long as he did. In the end, his mighty muscles were no match for his weak will. He caved and the Philistines quickly captured him.

> Freedom's enemies are waste, lethargy, indifference, immorality, and the insidious attitude of something for nothing.
>
> William Arthur Ward

Samson's downfall offers a stark portrayal of the true implications of moral compromise. Any one indiscretion may seem inconsequential or even insignificant. However, each time you dismiss a godly standard, the damage is real and potentially devastating in the long run.

Major moral missteps of tomorrow are established upon the minor misdeeds of today. Minimizing offenses or excusing ungodliness in any form is a cornerstone to justification of significant disobedience in the future. Just as Samson's enemies were able to capitalize upon his weaknesses because his long pattern of misbehavior made him an easy target, so, too, does continuing to indulge in moral compromise weaken you.

Samson was significantly blessed by God and powerfully used against his enemies. His feats were supernatural, but his lusts superseded his integrity. Ultimately, this is what made him powerless and drove him to his knees. Temptations can do the same to you if you do not learn from Samson.

Your strength is not in your hair or any physical element any more than was Samson's. Your strength is found in your faithful walk with God. Samson allowed his hair to be cut because he had placed his head in the lap of his enemy. Live in such a way that you do not find yourself similarly imperiled.

Keep your eyes open, hold tight to your convictions, give it all you've got, be resolute.

1 Corinthians 16:13 MSG

How Others
See It

No person is immune from moral compromise, even those who are otherwise upright and honorable. This was certainly the case with Samson, as E. W. Sprague suggests in *All the Spiritualism of the Christian Bible and the Scripture Directly Opposing It*:

"Samson was miraculously conceived by the edict of 'the angel of the Lord,' and was 'moved by the Spirit of the Lord,' and often 'the Spirit of the Lord came upon him,' controlling him. These high spiritual associations did not keep him walking in the pathway of moral rectitude."

Accordingly Kent and Barbara Hughes offer counsel to spiritual people today in their book *Liberating Ministry from the Success Syndrome*:

"Many of God's servants who have once responded to the call of God and committed themselves to a holy life and went forth with great expectation have fallen to sensuality. . . . Even more tragic is that they admit no inconsistency in their behavior. How Samson-like! But God's Word stands: all is failure apart from holiness."

Zooming **In**

The Nazirite vow that Samson's mother invoked upon him as a boy was a pledge to be set apart for the priesthood. As such, Samson was required to abstain from alcohol, never to cut his hair or beard, and never to be defiled by touching a corpse.

Because of Samson's exploits, he became one of the judges of Israel. His primary responsibility was to issue justice on behalf of the oppressed people of the land. The judges are remembered historically for their strong presence and for bringing Israel's confessions and regrets before God.

> *Moral compromise is often the predecessor to total collapse. Take the initial steps today to guard against compromise and failure.*

How have small indiscretions in your past led to larger offenses? In what ways did a small disobedience make a larger disobedience easier?

_____

_____

_____

_____

Enemies lay in wait for Samson, looking for opportunities to trap him. What are some traps that exist in your life that you need to be careful to avoid?

_____

_____

_____

_____

Samson mistakenly thought his strength was in his hair. To what have you incorrectly attributed your strength and character? Why is it important that you find your strength in God, rather than in yourself?

_____

_____

_____

Behaving Like a Baby

They were bringing children to Him so that He might touch them; but the disciples rebuked them. But when Jesus saw this, He was indignant and said to them, "Permit the children to come to Me; do not hinder them; for the kingdom of God belongs to such as these. Truly I say to you, whoever does not receive the kingdom of God like a child will not enter it at all." And He took them in His arms and began blessing them, laying His hands on them.

Mark 10:13–16 NASB

The Big Picture

By all accounts, Jesus loved children. The Bible records that children were often in the crowds where he spoke and performed miracles. He met them and eagerly received them, and as in the case of the boy with the fishes and loaves of bread, included them in his supernatural service to the throngs of people. He was sensitive particularly to the weak and feeble children and had compassion in healing them. He felt at ease around children, and children wanted to be around him.

The Bible records in Mark 10 that people were bringing their children to Jesus so that he might touch them. There is no telling what they desired from Jesus and his special touch. Perhaps their children had illnesses that they believed only Jesus could heal. Perhaps they hoped that some of Jesus' power would rub off on their children. Whatever the motivation, these parents brought their children to Jesus, and they ran to him.

The disciples were dismayed by the situation. Jesus was constantly being pressed into service, continually being tested by his enemies, and never seemed to find a moment to rest. Now—finally—it seemed like he might have such an opportunity for rest, and he instead found himself surrounded by needy, clamoring children, being egged on by their needy, clamoring parents.

Yet the moment the disciples attempted to put some distance between these children and the Messiah, Jesus took advantage of another teachable moment. He chastised the disciples for discouraging the children's initiative. Then, he told the crowd that these children demonstrated how all people should live. Just as every child rushed to Jesus simply to spend time with the Christ and be in his presence, so, too, should every person eagerly approach God to likewise spend time with him and be in his presence.

Jesus was not content to voice his lesson in terms of advice; he declared the absolute necessity of having the same disposition of these children. No person can approach God as though he is an equal, colleague, or peer. God must be approached with reverence, respect, and trust.

The essence of religion consists in the feeling of an absolute dependence.

Friedrich Schleiermacher

As the children flocked around the Messiah, his apostles apparently were not awestruck by how cute the children were and how precious they appeared surrounding their Lord. They saw the children's approach as an invasion of Jesus' time; in their opinion, Jesus had better things to do. But Jesus disagreed; he stated that all should come to him as these children had done.

A closer look shows that coming to Jesus as a child has less to do with approaching him in innocence than it does with admitting need and dependence. When the children approached Jesus, they did so with their own needs, interests, and desires in mind. They wanted to be with him. They wanted to have his attention. They wanted to hear him speak or to receive his healing touch. They did not care what the apostles wanted. They did not care where Jesus had been, what he had done, or how tired or hungry he may have been. The point was, they saw Jesus, and they wanted him. It was just that simple.

When the apostles tried to shoo the children away to relieve Jesus, he rebuked them. Jesus commended the children for approaching him with simplicity and purity in their motives. They had no complex schemes or ulterior motives. They simply wanted to be in the presence of the Christ, and nothing else mattered.

> *Innocence dwells with wisdom, but never with ignorance.*
>
> William Blake

You can learn a lot from the faith of a child who is untainted by years of experience and is not jaded by cynicism. True faith is born in the simplicity of need, uncomplicated by the impurities of conditional circumstance. Adults like to complicate what God makes simple. Children are typically straightforward about their needs, unhindered by

Apply It to Your Life

the shame that comes through years of guilt. If you tell a child she cannot get to heaven without Jesus, she is likely simply to go to Jesus. You share the same message with an adult, and she is more likely to expend tremendous effort to try to disprove the claim before agreeing that the claim is true.

Religious people may try to get you to schedule your time with God or to polish your approach. Thankfully, God requires neither of these practices. God wants you to bring your needs to him with a simplicity of heart, without the complications of excuse or condition. God is far less concerned with why you need him than he is with the simple reality that you do in fact need him. As Jesus showed, he is eager to receive you and even requires this unrefined approach. God desires you to share your needs sincerely, not strategically.

The poor and the needy will celebrate and shout because of the LORD, the holy God of Israel.

Isaiah 29:19 CEV

Jesus consistently taught that approaching God required humility; even humility expressed in the need of a child for the Father's provision. James Montgomery Boice wrote in *Christ's Call to Discipleship*:

"We would think the disciples would get the point, especially since it had been reinforced visually. But in the very next chapters . . . we see the disciples actually turning children aside. They have been telling their mothers that Jesus is too important, too busy. But really they are thinking that *they* are too busy. Besides, any time spent by Jesus on the children would be time not spent on them. Jesus was indignant with the disciples. He said, 'Let the children come to me, do not hinder them.' . . . Earlier Jesus had spoken on relative positions in his kingdom—the first would be last and the last first. Now he was teaching that without humility, it was not possible even to enter the kingdom."

Zooming **In**

The apostles were not trying to be rude in trying to usher away the children. They simply assumed they had a good idea of what Jesus needed to accomplish and also what he needed in order to accomplish it. They viewed the children as a distraction. Jesus viewed them as the reason why he had left heaven in the first place.

Children were not typically important citizens in the days of Jesus, but he paid particular attention to children. In addition to welcoming them into his audience, Jesus regularly interacted with children. He provided miracles to children and even used the lunch of the boy with two fish and a few loaves of bread to miraculously feed the massive crowd that was following him in those days.

One of the most misquoted statements ever incorrectly attributed to the Bible says, "God helps those who help themselves." The reality is, God most eagerly helps those who admit they need God's help.

Through the
Eyes of
Your Heart

What are you facing in your life that you cannot handle on your own? How would you like God to help you?

_____

_____

_____

_____

How does it make you feel to depend upon God like a child? What does this tell you about a person's sufficiency apart from God?

_____

_____

_____

_____

How are you tempted to be independent from God? What would be easier if you trusted God to handle it?

_____

_____

_____

_____

Life-and-Death Decisions

This day I call heaven and earth as witnesses against you that I have set before you life and death, blessings and curses. Now choose life, so that you and your children may live and that you may love the LORD your God, listen to his voice, and hold fast to him. For the LORD is your life, and he will give you many years in the land he swore to give to your fathers, Abraham, Isaac and Jacob.

Deuteronomy 30:19–20 NIV

The Big Picture

Moses was a leader with incredible patience. He had a seemingly impossible task—moving a nation from oppressive slavery and delivering it to its promised land of hope and freedom—and performed his task with wisdom, perseverance, and tolerance. The people who followed Moses were continually griping and complaining. They repeatedly questioned his judgment and argued against his decisions. Yet they also thought little of begging him to intercede with God on their behalf, asking for more food, more water, or just more blessing.

Year after year, situation after situation, the people of Israel had wavered between utter dependence on and near rebellion against Moses' leadership. Now the time was coming when Moses would no longer lead them. He was approaching the end of his life, and he had one final message to leave the people he had bravely led for forty years.

He reminded them of all they had experienced over the past four decades. They had witnessed miracles of deliverance and miracles of provision. They had seen the clothing and sandals miraculously withstand the wear of the years. They had seen food and quail rain from heaven, and water spring forth unexplainably from rocks. They had confronted bigger, stronger, larger, and more equipped enemies, and had defeated them.

In short, God had kept his promise. He had pledged to provide a land for his people. He was providing them a home where they could build their future, and where they could prosper. He had made a covenant with them, and he had kept his word regarding what he would do for them. He kept the promise because of who he is.

Before he allowed them to advance into their land, though, God warned them of the temptations that would await them. There would be more enemies. There would be opportunities to forget what they had seen from God, and what they knew about God. They would meet strangers who did not know God and who would lead Israel away from God if they had the opportunity.

In what lay ahead of Israel, God foretold of a blessing and a curse. Over forty years, God had equipped them with everything they needed to survive and thrive in the land he was giving to them. All they had to do was choose the blessings he had prepared for them. If they wanted to experience the fullness of God's good plan, they only had to remain close to him. The choice was theirs.

If you are unwilling to serve the LORD, then choose today whom you will serve. Would you prefer the gods your ancestors served beyond the Euphrates? Or will it be the gods of the Amorites in whose land you now live? But as for me and my family, we will serve the LORD.

Joshua 24:15 NLT

This Old Testament passage reminds us that God's people always vacillate between God's will and their own desires. Take a closer look at the encouraging message from God through Moses; decision making is easier when viewed from a perspective of whether or not the option gives life or takes it away.

The people of Israel were a population well conditioned to base their decisions—independently and corporately—according to the results of a cost-and-benefit analysis. They had weighed the risk of leaving Egypt with Moses against the high price of remaining in slavery to the pharaoh and decided that the benefits of the promised land were worth the risk. While they complained about Moses in the desert, they weighed the risk of returning or going out on their own against leaving his leadership and determined to stay. Now, on the verge of stepping into the fulfillment of all that God had long been promising them, they again faced a decision. This time, though, Moses put the options in the clearest terms possible.

If Israel was going to follow God, they needed to understand that their decision would bring life. To forge out on their own was to choose death. The language was extreme, but never more accurate. Without God, they would have no protection against their enemies and no chance at survival. With God, though, they had the promise of hope, provision, and a future.

> *Nobody ever did, or ever will, escape the consequences of his choices.*
>
> Alfred A. Montapert

Every day, God offers you opportunities to follow him, or for you to forge out on your own. Every day, the implications of your choice are the same. Any time you choose to live independently from God, you choose an option that is tainted by the stench of death. Any time you choose the option that trusts in God or relies upon God, you choose the option that is blessed with life.

Apply It
to Your Life

It may be difficult to view seemingly trifling choices in such dramatic terms. Nonetheless, every choice you make affirms either that God is sovereign or that you are the woefully lost captain of your own ship. If your life is in dire straits, it could be because you have spent too much time trying to wrest control of a helm you were never destined or skilled enough to captain. The best course of action is to change course and give control over to God. This action is nothing less than choosing life over death.

Finally, following God not only gives life, but it also gives generations of blessings. When your life responds to God's leading, it points others to him as well. An independent life only points to a dead end that begins and concludes with yourself. Choose life today for you and all who come behind you.

Anyone who chooses to be a friend of the world becomes an enemy of God.

James 4:4 NIV

Success in life is not merely choosing right; it is also submitting to righteousness. Henry Cloud and John Townsend wrote in *12 "Christian" Beliefs That Can Drive You Crazy: Relief from False Assumptions*:

"Equally important to our choices is submitting to God and to his church for support and absorbing his Word and his truth. Through relationships we forge in the body of Christ, we must confess the deep aspects of our heart. We must learn to depend on God's Spirit to discover what is choking our spiritual growth. . . . And then we must practice what we are learning."

Peter J. Gomes, in *Strength for the Journey: Biblical Wisdom for Daily Living*, wrote:

"God gives the freedom to choose the ultimate, the best, the highest. You are free to choose God. . . . Therefore it is simple; give all that you are and have to him who is worthy of all you are and have. Give to God nothing less than your whole life and all that is in it and within it, and then you will be truly free. Make the right choice, and then you will know the freedom that is perfect service."

Zooming **In**

The choices that Moses pressed Israel to make concerned their spiritual devotion to God alone as Lord expressed through their willingness to follow him, or not. There was no middle ground, only the opportunity to choose life or death. To help Israel remember all that God had accomplished, Moses recounted God's exploits of provision, protection, deliverance, and blessing.

Moses offered this choice to Israel as they faced crossing the Jordan into the promised land. In receiving this message in this context, the message clearly spoke to Israel that they would need to completely rely upon God to prosper in this new land as they faced foreign people and flawed beliefs. On their own, they would be overtaken and ultimately defeated. With God's help, though, they would blossom and enjoy blessing.

Every decision you make either adds to your life or takes away from it. Choose wisely when it comes time to make your next decision.

What is a decision you have made in the past that has taken away from your quality of life? What have you learned from that? What are you doing differently?

_____

_____

_____

What is a decision you have made in the past that has added to your quality of life? How has that affected other relationships?

_____

_____

_____

What is a decision you are facing in the immediate future? What can you see about particular options that either adds to or takes away from your quality of life?

_____

_____

_____

_____

Best in Show

Let each one examine his own work, and then he will have rejoicing in himself alone, and not in another.

Galatians 6:4 NKJV

The Big Picture

The Bible's book of Galatians emphasizes the liberty that God offers. Liberty was a precious but rare commodity in New Testament times. A semblance of liberty existed for these communities where Jewish and Roman authority combined to exert definition on the cultures they controlled. Citizens enjoyed limited freedoms as long as they followed the civic laws of Rome as pagans, or the religious laws of the Old Testament as Jewish citizens.

Paul, though, introduced true liberty when he ushered the advent of Christianity into the region. Due to an illness that restricted his travel while on a missionary journey, Paul invested an extended time in Galatia and nearby Phrygia where he preached the gospel and taught about salvation by faith in Jesus. Those who were converted to Christianity learned a revolutionary concept about liberty—it is not the right or ability to do whatever one chooses; it is the right and ability to do what God desires.

Some time after Paul's departure, the liberating message of Jesus was compromised in the Galatian church. People known as Judaizers began to infiltrate the emerging Christian church. Judaizers believed that Christianity was acceptable, but only if the Old Testament laws recorded by Moses remained in effect. Accordingly, they required all new believers—even non-Jewish converts—to adhere to those laws of sacrifice and ceremony in order to belong to the church.

Paul reminded the Galatians what life was like before knowing the real freedom God offers. They remembered what life was like when they had to pay tributes to the controlling authorities and offer homage to the political powers. He reiterated that no religious ritual or legalistic ceremony could put a person in right standing before God. They had right standing with God because of what Jesus had done for them on the cross.

In this, the Galatians finally had freedom. They were not controlled by external measures. Their acceptance by God was not based upon how well they obeyed certain laws or if they behaved better than their neighbor. They could reflect upon their own lives, free from comparison, and see that God's grace alone put them in good standing with their Creator. Their joy was complete because they had liberty through Christ, and not at the expense of another person.

Do all the good you can, by all the means you can, in all the ways you can, in all the places you can, at all the times you can, to all the people you can, as long as ever you can.

John Wesley

Take a
Closer Look

A closer look at this brief verse highlights the reality that life's grade is not on a sliding scale. Paul reminded the Galatians not to be overly focused on the conduct, behavior, or even the accomplishments of others because God's favor had nothing to do with their performance in respect to their contemporaries. The Galatian church needed to understand that their standing with God had nothing do with whether they were as holy as other churches or even holier because they adopted the extra rites of the Judaizers. They needed to embrace the reality that God accepted them based upon the perfect work that he had accomplished on the cross and nothing more. They could not add to his favor by adding rituals and practices, no matter how sanctimonious. If they would simply take God at his word and trust him, God would be pleased.

Little has changed in two thousand years. Virtually every religion offers extrabiblical traditions that convey an added element of sanctity or righteousness. Regardless of the tradition or practice, the final measure of your standing before God is whether or not you will be standing before God alone, or in the company of Jesus, who is the mediator between God and man.

Flirst learn to love yourself, then you can love me.

Saint Bernard of Clairvaux

Today's world has people always trying to keep up with the Joneses or trying to be as good or better than the next guy. This is as true in the spiritual world as it is in the secular realm. Any way that a church can chart commitment—by attendance, participation, or by giving—is a measure that can be inappropriately used as a false standard of accomplishment.

Apply It
to Your Life

The good news is that you are not judged according to an attendance roll or a financial report. You are judged by your faith in Jesus, and nothing more. The great thing about knowing that faith in Jesus is the absolute standard for being accepted by God is that now you are freed to do and give all you can for more important reasons than trying to earn God's favor. Now you can give and serve because you already have the promise of God's full favor, rather than trying to accumulate it on your own.

When you adopt God's absolute standard, your joy abounds because everything is celebrated in abundance. You never have to worry if you have done enough. Rejoice that in Christ, every effort is pleasing to God.

Godliness with contentment is great gain.
1 Timothy 6:6 NIV

How Others
See It

The danger of boasting is that it distorts the quality of the work and destroys the effect of it too. Martin Luther wrote in *Epistle to the Galatians*:

"The Apostle has in mind the work of the ministry. The problem with these seekers is that they never stop to consider whether their ministry is straightforward and faithful. All they think about is whether people will like them or praise them. . . . A faithful minister cares little what people think of him, as long as his conscience approves him. . . . To preach the gospel for praise is bad business especially when people stop praising you. Find your praise in the testimony of a clean conscience. This passage may be applied to other works than the ministry. The best commendation of any work is to know that one has done the work that God has given him well and that God is pleased with his effort."

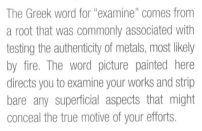

Zooming **In**

The Greek word for "examine" comes from a root that was commonly associated with testing the authenticity of metals, most likely by fire. The word picture painted here directs you to examine your works and strip bare any superficial aspects that might conceal the true motive of your efforts.

The notion that a people would keep their boasting to themselves was as counterintuitive to the culture of Galatia as it seems today. Paul was familiar with the human inclination to self-promote. He knew what boasting afforded to those who did it. Paul therefore encouraged people that if they were to boast, to do so unto God, so that God's reputation would benefit rather than the person's.

If you run a race, you cannot have any hope of winning if all your attention is on the performance of others. Focus on your efforts, and trust God to give you commendation.

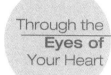

Through the
Eyes of
Your Heart

Have you ever been jealous at the success of another? What was it about his or her success that was difficult for you to accept?

_____

_____

_____

How has God used you in a unique way? How did you give God credit for doing so?

_____

_____

_____

What are you doing right now that is pleasing to God? What is your motivation for doing this? How can you build upon this?

_____

_____

_____

_____

Heart Problems

Jacob was left alone, and a man wrestled with him until daybreak. When the man saw that He could not defeat him, He struck Jacob's hip as they wrestled and dislocated his hip socket. Then He said to Jacob, "Let Me go, for it is daybreak." But Jacob said, "I will not let You go unless You bless me." "What is your name?" the man asked. "Jacob!" he replied.

Genesis 32:24–27 HCSB

The Big Picture

There is really no reason to sugarcoat it. Jacob was a troublemaker. He had been this way since the day he entered the world, hanging on the heel of his twin brother, Esau. As a young man, he cleverly outwitted his older brother out of his birthright, and later deceived his father, Isaac, into giving him Esau's blessing. Out of fear for his own life because of his dishonesty, Jacob fled from home rather than risk being killed by his furious brother.

Jacob was the type of guy who found trouble, even when he was not making trouble. When he finally arrived in Paddan Aram, he fell in love at first sight with Rachel. He immediately determined to marry her, and her father, Laban, agreed that if Jacob would labor for seven years, he could indeed have her as his wife. On the morning after their wedding, Jacob awoke to find Leah, not Rachel, asleep by his side. In exchange for another seven years of labor, Jacob was able to take Rachel as his bride.

take a CLOSER look

Now this man, who had lived his life by deception, lived with the fruit of having been deceived by his father-in-law. On the run from an enraged brother, he was now the husband to two wives and had a father-in-law and employer who could not be trusted. To make matters more complicated, Rachel was infertile while Leah gave Jacob four sons in succession. In desperation, Rachel gave her maidservant to Jacob and produced two sons whom Rachel claimed as her own. Then, Leah followed that example by giving her own maidservant, and giving him two more sons. Leah eventually birthed three more children, and Rachel herself birthed a son, Joseph. By the time the supper table was set, Jacob had twelve children (eleven boys and one girl) by four women. And he was still on the lam.

A man with family demands, Jacob made an agreement with his father-in-law that certain spotted, speckled, and dark animals would become Jacob's while the others would belong to Laban. God blessed Jacob's flock, and their numbers increased to a much greater degree than the numbers of Laban's flock. This made his father-in-law angry, so Jacob packed up his family, gathered his flocks, and left. Again, Jacob was on the run. This time, though, he had to run back in the direction from which he had come. He would have to confront his brother, Esau. He sent his family away for safety. That night, alone and with his back to the shore of the Jabbok ford, he went to sleep fearful that his life of deception had finally caught up to him.

Falsehood is easy, truth so difficult.
George Eliot

Take a
Closer Look

Jacob's wrestling match with God on the riverbank is a well-known story often related to the struggle for truth. A closer look at this story shows that wrestling with God really means coming to terms with the deeply deceptive nature of your own heart.

When he grappled with God, Jacob was forced to confess his own name. This meant more than just identifying himself. More than that, Jacob had to admit that all the way down to his nature, he was a deceiver.

This was a profound admission, backed up by the facts of his life. Everything that Jacob had accomplished and earned through his entire life was gained through deceptive means. He had both played the deceiver and been deceived, and the result was a life in turmoil filled with contention. Such a confession was necessary for him in order to see a much-needed change become a reality in his life.

As the Scripture illustrates, such a struggle can be monumental. The contest took the entire night, and even after the admission, Jacob continued to rely upon the dishonest and comfortably deceptive practices of his past. Even so, the key event in his life was coming to terms with the depths of his nature as a deceiver and admitting to God that on his own, he could not be trusted.

Nobody deceives us better than we deceive ourselves.

Seneca

You might be tempted to say, "I am nothing like Jacob!" However, the Bible declares that every human heart is deceitful above all things and cannot be trusted. Whether you have told only a few lies in your life or whether you have a reputation as a lying scoundrel, the deceptive nature of your heart is universally untrustworthy.

Apply It
to Your Life

This does not make you a bad person. It just makes you a person in need of a new heart, spiritually speaking. Just as God changed Jacob's name to Israel (which appropriately means "struggles with God"), reflecting his new nature, so, too, does God desire to give you a new nature that is free from self-deceit. You may find yourself with your back against the wall having to wrestle with God in order to receive this blessing, but it is a necessary experience.

Jacob discovered that confessing his old nature was required to receive God's blessing. The same thing is true for us. Only pride in the old nature stands in the way of declaring a similar self-disclosure. Jacob determined that the pain of holding on to his old nature was more unbearable than the unknown of what would happen when he confessed to God. The pleasant result was blessing, for himself, his family, and all of Israel. God offers the same opportunity to you today, if you will just admit your true nature to him.

Putting aside all malice and all deceit and hypocrisy and envy and all slander, like newborn babies, long for the pure milk of the word, so that by it you may grow in respect to salvation, if you have tasted the kindness of the Lord.

1 Peter 2:1–3 NASB

That God would meet Jacob for an all-night struggle shows that God is not afraid of getting hands-on to help a person come to terms with who they are. Mike Tucker said:

"God the father allows his children to wrestle with him. He allows us to shove our difficulties and perplexities and anger and demands right in his face. The odds of winning a wrestling match against God are not great, of course. But we try all the time. . . . Jacob was the type of person who wanted everything and wanted it now. He did not want to give in to God. But God's plans were so much better than anything he could have come up with, and he needed to acknowledge that. . . . Do you find yourself wrestling with God today? The truth is, the only way to win in this life is to lose to God. We have to give up. When we submit our entire lives to his will, we ensure ourselves genuine success."

Zooming **In**

The word translated "Jacob" in Hebrew means "heel-catcher" or "deceiver." For Jacob, both descriptions fit. He emerged from his mother's womb clasping the heel of his brother, Esau, and developed a fitting reputation as a perpetual deceiver.

A famous Scripture from the book of Jeremiah speaking to the deceptive nature of every person's heart uses this same root word to describe the heart's malady. Truly, the man who would one day be known as Israel, as the father of a nation, was born with deception coursing through his nature.

It has been said that confession is not telling God what he already knows, but it is coming to a point of agreement with what God says is truth.

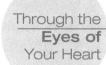

Have you been in denial regarding any unwholesome personal conduct? Why is it important to view your conduct from God's perspective?

_____

_____

_____

_____

Have you ever figuratively "wrestled with God"? What were the effects of that experience?

_____

_____

_____

_____

How has God given you a new nature? What has he changed in you that allows you to tell others that God is in the work of changing lives?

_____

_____

_____

_____

_____

It Takes a Church

Let us not neglect our meeting together, as some people do, but encourage and warn each other, especially now that the day of his coming back again is drawing near.

Hebrews 10:25 NLT

The Big Picture

The first church leaders had a common strategy whenever they took the gospel into a new region. First, they would visit the local synagogues and over a period of several Sabbaths, they would reason with the local rabbis about the legitimacy of Jesus as the Messiah of God. As they effectively shared the gospel in the synagogue and won converts, they would then expand their efforts to persuade non-Jewish people in the community. They would go wherever they could find people willing to listen, most often beginning in the public forums.

Because Hebrew people were the object of their initial effort, the early church consisted of a large number of converts from Judaism. Accordingly, there was a constant tension among these Jewish converts as they rethought everything they had understood about God. Much of this rethinking had to do with the infusion of the radical concept of grace: that they could not increase the pleasure or favor of God by their external efforts at being religious.

This new tension was evident in the challenge they faced in developing a new understanding of corporate worship. The synagogue was where Jewish believers gathered for prayer and for learning the Old Testament Scriptures. The temple existed for the rituals of sin sacrifice, priestly intercession, and religious festivals and celebrations. Believing Jesus is God's Messiah required these converts to understand that this new belief meant Jesus made the ultimate sacrifice for their offenses against God, and they no longer needed to go to the temple for that purpose.

Receiving Jesus as Lord also meant believing that God's Holy Spirit would dwell within them. Because of this, they were no longer reliant upon a priest to mediate between them and God.

The biblical letter to Hebrew believers invests considerable effort to affirm these doctrines. Explaining these new beliefs helped people understand the complexity of who Jesus was, and the depth and breadth of what Jesus accomplished on the cross, but in doing so, a new inquest was opened.

If Jesus fulfilled their spiritual needs and his sacrifice made going to the temple unnecessary, then why gather with other Christians at all? The answer then was the same as it is today. The church is not a building to house religious rituals. It is a home for people of faith, learning *from* one another and *with* one another how to put that faith into practice, so that Sunday words match their actions the other six days of the week.

The religious community is essential, for alone our
vision is too narrow to see all that must be seen.
Together, our vision widens and strength is renewed.

Mark Morrison-Reed

Take a
Closer Look

Many people today dismiss church as a viable way to grow in their faith. "It is filled with hypocrites!" is a common defense. A closer look at this verse shows that this complaint is accurate! However, this is the exact reason why church is necessary. God gives the church to the hypocrites so they may warn and encourage one another to become less so as they grow together.

If the church forbade admittance to hypocrites, then no person would ever be able to enter a church at all. Every person struggles with hypocrisy on some level. For some people, the hypocrisy is small or segmented. They may compartmentalize their lives in such a way that conduct in one segment is completely different from another, and appropriate in one, but not another. Other people struggle with hypocrisy on a monumental level, where there seems to be no consistency in any one relationship or environment, much less all of them.

So for all the hypocrites of the world, God offers the church. It is where double talk can be corrected and single truth is exemplified. Double-mindedness is refuted and rebuked in the church, but celebrated in the world. The world is ill with a plague of hypocrisy. Church allows hypocrites to bring their weakness before God in community. Community builds faith and cures hypocrisy.

> *Church isn't where you meet. Church isn't a building. Church is what you do. Church is who you are. Church is the human outworking of the person of Jesus Christ. Let's not go to church, let's be the church.*
>
> Bridget Willard

You likely do not have to think very hard before you can remember a person whose opinion voiced in Sunday church did not exactly match up with their conduct on the following Friday night. There is no such thing as a perfect church, so there is no sense in holding out for one.

However, God himself has declared that the church, with all its imperfections, is the best place to gather with others to be encouraged and exhorted. The best churches allow people to be honest about their shortcomings and transparent with their needs. You have the opportunity as a Christian to find that sort of church or to help the church you are in to be that sort of church.

The church will be perfect when you get to heaven. There will be no more hypocrisy when you begin your eternal life. Until then, bear the burdens of your fellow Christ followers with grace, gentleness, and mercy, and do your best to live a life of authenticity as an example to those who struggle with being genuine.

Praise the LORD! Sing to the LORD a new song, and His praise in the assembly of saints.

Psalm 149:1 NKJV

Gathering as "an assembly" not only allows for encouragement and warning, but it brings together people for the sake of directing attention toward God in worship. Everett Ferguson wrote in *The Church of Christ: A Biblical Ecclesiology for Today*:

"The assembly of Christians is part of their total service to God. . . . The church in assembly not only provides encouragement to others, but also approaches God."

In *When God Builds a Church: 10 Principles for Growing a Dynamic Church*, Bob Russell adds:

"You ought to attend weekly worship even when you do not feel like going. Your presence might be an encouragement to another believer who has come to be uplifted. And you need to be edified too!"

Zooming In

The first churches where Jesus was worshiped looked much different from the congregations today. The Christians of the first church met almost daily, sharing meals together and spending significant time together as they searched the Scriptures to understand God and to serve others. Their growth was primarily in the context of this community.

The sentence structure of this passage in the original language offers repeated contrasts that help shape understanding of what a church has to offer believers today. The pairing to "not neglect . . . but encourage" illustrates that church is not simply a home for worshiping God—which can be done anywhere—but it is also a gathering point for believers to be strengthened in their faith.

Church was never meant to be dull, dry, or dreary. Rediscover what is good about church and make every effort to have gathering with other Christians be a common activity in your life.

Through the
Eyes of
Your Heart

Why do you go to church? What is your favorite aspect of going to church?

What are some things that you can do at or through your church that you cannot do anywhere else?

Who are some of your friends from church? How are you strengthened and encouraged by their friendship?

Calling God

"You said, 'No, we will get our help from Egypt. They will give us swift horses for riding into battle.' But the only swiftness you are going to see is the swiftness of your enemies chasing you! One of them will chase a thousand of you. Five of them will make all of you flee. You will be left like a lonely flagpole on a distant mountaintop." But the LORD still waits for you to come to him so he can show you his love and compassion. For the LORD is a faithful God. Blessed are those who wait for him to help them. O people of Zion, who live in Jerusalem, you will weep no more. He will be gracious if you ask for help. He will respond instantly to the sound of your cries.

Isaiah 30:16–19 NLT

The Big Picture

The nation of Israel had a relationship with God that seemed to go through more cycles than a washing machine at a public Laundromat. The nation went through periods where it was acutely interested in the will of God and strove hard to obey God. They worshiped him. They kept the law and flourished under his provision. Despite the faithful blessings the people enjoyed, those times cyclically gave way to periods where Israel instead chose to ignore or even disobey God. The Israelites would evaluate a circumstance and choose to follow their own wisdom rather than rely on God. Inevitably, when they chose this route, they regretted doing so.

Such was the case when, in Isaiah 30, Israel's plan to form a partnership with Egypt in response to the threat of invasion by the Assyrians raised the wrath of God. Virtually every time they faced the threat of war or invasion, rather than turning to God and trusting him for their defense, Israel plotted and built alliances with neighboring countries.

From a human perspective, such alliances were strategic and made good sense. They would trust in the might of a neighbor, covering their own weaknesses with their new ally's strength. This would also build camaraderie between the two nations and allow for future prosperity in trade and diplomacy. They would use the resources of their neighbor—resources they themselves did not possess—and if everything worked out as they had hoped, they would thwart the invasion while building for their future.

Reliance on foreign powers came at a great expense, too. They loaded gold and riches upon the backs of camels, transporting it to their potential allies to buy their loyalty. They gambled that these payments were an investment in their own future; and they would rather pay a king's ransom than risk facing the enemy on their own.

Israel's real problem was they never counted the even greater cost, which is what angered God. To trust in Egypt, Israel decided to distrust God. It also meant that they must compromise themselves spiritually to have close ties with the nation of Egyptians who worshiped false gods. Those false beliefs and wayward practices invariably polluted the worship of Israel. While many citizens, leaders, and strategists determined that they were simply covering all their options to keep Assyria at bay, God rightly perceived that Israel's actions were nothing less than spiritual betrayal. When Israel stopped relying upon God alone for their safety and prosperity, God allowed them to experience the painful consequences of that foolishness.

God is our mighty fortress, always ready to help in times of trouble.

Psalm 46:1 CEV

A closer look at this passage illustrates that when you make a bad situation worse by following your own limited wisdom, God waits for you to come back to him with your needs, and he will immediately answer with grace and provision.

Israel had no business forming an alliance with Egypt. The two nations had long histories of opposition. They had different belief systems and different cultural practices. Remember, too, that Egypt had enslaved Israel for generations, simply because the people of Israel had grown numerous while living in Egypt. Yet the common fear of the approaching Assyrians caused them to put those significant details aside. Israel chose to disregard everything that God was telling them through the prophet Isaiah and determined that a partnership with Egypt was logical, strategic, and appropriate.

Despite all the earthly evidence that led to this decision, God omnisciently informed them that their choice would end in utter defeat. Their ally would flee. Their people would be overrun. Their efforts would fail. God permitted this because Israel's plan was the evidence of their lack of faith in him to protect them. Nonetheless, when they learned the lesson of the futility of self-preservation, he offered himself to his people. They could find him and return to him, and he would forgive them, meet their needs, and overcome their foes.

> *The best prayers have often more groans than words.*
>
> John Bunyan

When you find yourself facing a problem, you will have no lack of so-called experts who can tell you how to fix it. You have little in common with them, but they are available . . . at a cost that is often more than financial.

All the while, God is available. He desires to be your first option. He desires to meet your needs for protection, for provision, for overcoming, and for success. People too often look to God only when every one of their plans and connivances fails. Too often, you have to pay high interest, expensive fees, pricey retainers, and incalculable costs only to be right where you were before, or even worse for the experience. Too often, it is only when every other option fails that people go to God in prayer asking for his solution to their predicaments.

The good news is that he patiently waits for you. He loves you and is available to meet your needs. He will immediately respond to you. Trust in him, and remember that you do not have to prove your inability to fix everything before you ask him to take over. He already knows and has a plan that will make everything better.

Don't you think God will surely give justice to his chosen people who plead with him day and night? Will he keep putting them off? I tell you, he will grant justice to them quickly!

Luke 18:7–8 NLT

God will show you his options for your needs if you ask him to reveal them. Ruth Graham writes in her book *In Every Pew Sits a Broken Heart: Hope for the Hurting*:

"Are you in a crisis of great magnitude? Cry out to God in your pain. Be honest with him about what you are feeling. Ask him to reveal himself to you. Try to see those who are helping you in your life right now as being God's own instruments. See God as the source; depend on him. He is helping you through others. Ask God to give you more faith so you can believe him for the impossible. Do you believe God really wants to help you? Ask God to help you in the dark."

Patrick Morley wrote in *The Man in the Mirror*:

"God will help you. . . . He is not so much interested in your position as he is your attitude, in where you are as in where you are going. . . . We all do exactly what we decide in our minds to do. We can decide with or without God's help, but he promises to always help us if we trust in him."

Zooming **In**

Isaiah represented God to his people in a time that was rife with civil division, both internally and internationally. Isaiah primarily spoke against ungodly behavior in the Southern Kingdom of Judah (in the divided nation of Israel) and particularly in Jerusalem, but saw his king, Hezekiah, confirm the ill-conceived alliance with Egypt against the Assyrians when the prophet encouraged the king to resist their advances.

Isaiah was one of the noteworthy prophets who spoke on behalf of God in this era. Micah was a contemporary of Isaiah's, speaking against the ungodly behavior of the South. Prior to their efforts, Hosea, Amos, and Jonah were commissioned by God to speak against the North. Legend reports that Isaiah was killed due to the opposition of Manasseh, who succeeded Hezekiah, erected cultic temples, and slew anyone who opposed him in this.

take a CLOSER look

There are many times when God wants you to trust only him, rather than trying to find other solutions that will just leave you worse for the experience.

When have you seen a bad situation made worse by the solution that you thought would fix the original problem? What was it that made things worse?

_____

_____

_____

_____

Have you ever thought you could count on a person because of his or her reputation, only to find out otherwise? What did you learn from that experience?

_____

_____

_____

_____

This passage says that God will wait for you to return to him. When have you gone to a biblical solution to a problem only as a last resort? How did you see God meet that need?

_____

_____

_____

_____

Intelligent Design

Before I shaped you in the womb, I knew all about you. Before you saw the light of day, I had holy plans for you: A prophet to the nations—that is what I had in mind for you.

Jeremiah 1:5 MSG

The Big Picture

Jeremiah was a man completely humbled before God. Jeremiah was undoubtedly a religious man, as the son of a temple priest. He had a proper perspective of God and likely considered no higher honor than serving God with every day of his life.

As was the custom of the times, just such a prospect was his likely destiny. Most often, sons followed their father's vocational footsteps. Jeremiah was possibly already in training to one day join the priesthood. Every year, he accompanied his father on the three-mile trek from Anatoth to Jerusalem for the annual feasts. He observed his father administer in the temple, and possibly wondered if he, one day, would be repeating these same acts of preparation and intercession as a priest.

Without warning, one day in 628 BC, God spoke and changed all those plans. God revealed that he had made plans before Jeremiah was created in his mother's womb that this young man would be a prophet—a spokesman for God. The Lord had plans for him to leave behind the safe, predictable future in his father's household and instead relocate to Jerusalem where he would be the very voice of God to a nation that was known to rebel against and even revile similarly commissioned men in the past.

Ever since that day when God visited Jeremiah and shared his plans, people have been captivated by the notion that God knows everything about a person before he or she is ever born. Not only does God know what is in store for each person's life, but he has planned each and every event, detail, circumstance, and situation. This revolutionary truth confirms that life itself is no accident of nature and affirms that every experience has purpose and meaning.

God ordained for Jeremiah to be born at the right time, in the right place, to the right parents, in the right circumstance, for the right situation, to fulfill the purpose that God had planned for him before he ever saw the light of day. It was with the bold confidence of that provision that Jeremiah changed his plans to meet God's will and fulfill the plans that his Maker had created specifically for him.

To know the will of God is the greatest knowledge!
To do the will of God is the greatest achievement!

George W. Truett

This verse is often used as proof that God is the giver and originator of life and that every life is precious. A careful look at this verse takes the truth even further. Not only did God create you in your mother's womb, he cares for you so much that he had a plan for you in the works before you were even born.

Jeremiah—a priest-in-training—had to discover that God had a different plan for him than he or his family had been working toward his entire life. He had to learn that even a good plan is not the right plan if it is not God's plan. Jeremiah found himself confronted with a plan for his future that was different from his own, and he had to choose how to respond.

Jeremiah's obedient response to God is born in the understanding that God is the purposeful Creator of life. Jeremiah determined that because God had "knit" him together in his mother's womb, the Lord had done so for a purpose that was inextricably tied to a bigger plan and purpose. Jeremiah completely abandoned himself to the bigger plan of God and trusted that God's prepared place for him in that plan was far better than anything the man could have manufactured for himself, even as a priest.

> *I was raised to believe that God has a plan for everyone and that seemingly random twists of fate are all a part of His plan.*
>
> Ronald Reagan

God has a plan for you, too. You have a place in God's grand drama for world history. Your part may be small from an earthly perspective, but if you commit yourself to the part that God has prepared, you will fill the role that nobody else in the world can.

You may find yourself at a crossroad as you face the reality that God may have a plan for you that requires you to take a new direction other than the one you have been traveling your entire life to get you to this point. You may be happy doing what you have done—or maybe you are miserable—but if God's plan requires a change, you will be better for it and because of it.

Life is not random, and your life certainly is full of meaning. The meaning of your life is understood through fulfilling the general purpose God has for all people, and the specific plan he has expressly for you. That specific plan is the entire reason you were created, and you will spend your entire life discovering the details of that plan. You were knit together in your mother's womb with love and care so that you could enjoy the adventure of discovering the plan.

But the plans of the LORD stand firm forever, the purposes of his heart through all generations.

Psalm 33:11 NIV

Viewing life through the contextual lens of God's plan can help you decide which choices are necessary and which distract you from what God desires. In their book *Just for Girls,* Elizabeth M. Hoekstra and M. Beth Cutaiar write:

"God's plan for you is like a big picture book, huge, opened up in his lap. He has your life all planned out; it is already written in this book. Each colorful page shows you at different stages in your life. He knows and sees what will be happening in your life. . . . He wants you to flourish, to grow in mind, body, and spirit. His plan for you is exclusively yours. His plan for you was written in his big picture book before you were ever born. He knows you so well, better than your best friend, mom, or dad, that his plan is perfect for you!"

Tom Malone wrote in *What's Important: A Roadmap for Loving God*:

"God has a plan for you which extends beyond his plan for all of us, that we love him, obey his laws, love others, and do the right thing. God has a plan for you as an individual that requires you use your individual talents, gifts, abilities, interests, aptitudes, creativity and skills to love him, to witness to him, to make him known, to lead others to him, to love others, and to obey his commandments."

Zooming **In**

Jeremiah's name in Hebrew means "God throws." In perhaps his most ironic prophecy, Jeremiah warned the disobedient king of Israel, Jehoiakim, that God would roll him into a little ball and throw him out of Jerusalem. The king was overthrown and murdered, and his body was discarded without pomp or regard outside the gates of the city, where he was buried like a common farm animal.

Jeremiah was born in the early 600s BC, and he was known as "the weeping prophet" because of his lament over the sad spiritual condition of Israel. He is the attributed author of the Old Testament books Jeremiah and Lamentations. He repeatedly warned Israel about its impending defeat by Nebuchadnezzar of the Babylonians as a consequence for its ongoing disobedience to God. The warning became reality when Babylonia conquered Israel in 589 BC.

God has made a plan for you. Discovering his intentions for your life may cause you to change directions and allow you to finally proceed with confidence and clarity.

Have you ever struggled with what you wanted to do with your life? How do you feel to know God has specific plans for you?

_____

_____

_____

Have you ever felt as though God wants you to do something different than what you are currently doing? How would your life be different if you decided to do it?

_____

_____

_____

What will you have to give up to act on God's plan? What will you gain in doing so?

_____

_____

_____

_____

Cautious Counsel

God gives helpful advice to everyone who obeys him and protects all of those who live as they should. God sees that justice is done, and he watches over everyone who is faithful to him.

Proverbs 2:7–8 CEV

The Big Picture

The writer of most of the Bible's proverbial wisdom, King Solomon was a person of deep insight who possessed a treasure trove of life experience. By his own account, he had intentionally sought the meaning of life, searching for answers anywhere and everywhere possible. He indulged every whim. He welcomed every impulse. He satisfied every lust. He fulfilled every urge. He chased folly after frivolity in hopes of finding meaning and significance. He made many mistakes along the way and learned difficult lessons in the process.

However, one right move Solomon made was in asking God for wisdom above any other blessing. Accordingly, Solomon gained a reputation as the wisest man of his day, perhaps because of all he had learned by trial and error. Every venture, adventure, and misadventure added to Solomon's encyclopedia of insight. From these reserves, he became an open book, and shared that wisdom with others. Solomon's very name became synonymous with the prize of wisdom.

take a CLOSER look

Unfortunately, history also remembers Solomon as the king whose downfall arrived because he did not follow the wisdom he shared so freely with others. After offering several stanzas of levelheaded guidance about relationships, Solomon's reign was compromised by the multitude of foreign women he welcomed as brides. As they joined his extensive family affair, they brought with them their devotion to false gods and pagan practices. Before long, the wives' sway and influence decayed Solomon's loyalty to his own God who had blessed him with so much wisdom and wealth.

After exhorting others to bring up children who would cherish wisdom themselves, King Solomon failed to do so within his own family. When his own son Rehoboam later became king over Israel, it was the son's failure to heed the advice of wiser, older counsel that led to the country's division into two separate lands.

By his own pen Solomon acknowledges the faithfulness of God to liberally open the vault of wisdom, requiring only obedience. Logically, this reveals that God gives wisdom so that it can be used. When you apply God's advice to life, you experience wisdom, and the benefit of this wisdom is protection. Blessings are issued by the God who bestows wisdom. Without wisdom, you are unprotected from the merciless oppression of disobedient living. All you have to do is look at history and learn from King Solomon's mistakes.

Knowing your own strength is a fine thing.
Recognizing your own weakness is even better.
What is really bad, what hurts and finally defeats
us, is mistaking a weakness for a strength.

Sydney J. Harris

Every day, every person is challenged with decisions concerning right and wrong, good and better. A closer look at this proverb encourages those who do the right thing and walk with integrity, because God's protection and victory are promised.

Solomon had these promises and experienced the unmatched blessings of provision as the leader of Israel. However, later in life he turned his back on the very same wisdom God had given him. Accordingly, he turned away from the protection and victory he had grown accustomed to as a younger man.

When Solomon deferred to the insight of God, he reaped rewards and acclaim. His kingdom was revered and his holdings expanded. He exhibited discernment, good judgment, and insight as a leader, counselor, and mediator. He enjoyed renown that has survived for generations. The bounty bestowed upon him earlier in life had been established on a firm bedrock of reliance upon the wisdom of God.

Now he frittered it all away through a series of bad decisions regarding the very same matters he had spoken about earlier with authority and confidence. Between continually adding contentious women to his household and refusing to invest wisdom in his own children, Solomon would eventually pay the highest interest on the accrued debt of wisdom. His example reverberates today as a call to learn from his errors.

Many receive advice, only the wise profit from it.

Publilius Syrus

Solomon's example simply exhorts you to follow the wisdom that God freely offers through his
Word. God has pledged that if you will do what he
recommends that you do, he will bless you as he
has promised. If you choose to go down your own
path, the results are far more speculative.

Apply It
to Your Life

You may be able to identify some modern
Solomons as well. People who began well and experienced the blessings of
God over their business, their relationships, or their investments, only to lose
the very things that God had given them because later in life they turned their
back on what they knew and indulged in foolishness. People who used to
have it all, but now lament how they have lost it all.

Look around to see the folly of disregarding God's wisdom. Outrageous
debt. Fragmented families. Rebellious children. Devastating addictions. The
factor connecting protection with provision is found in obedience. Commit to
the principle that if God graciously imparts his wisdom to you and tells you
to do something, you will do it. No matter what. Even if it flies in the face of
what the world says is correct or fun.

*Wisdom or money can get you almost anything, but it's
important to know that only wisdom can save your life.*

Ecclesiastes 7:12 NLT

The Bible declares that "the fear of the LORD is the beginning of wisdom" (Proverbs 9:10 NKJV). When that healthy respect for the might of God dissipates, wisdom gained is likely to be lost. J. Sidlow Baxter wrote in his book *Baxter's Explore the Book*:

"The sun of Solomon's glory set in dark clouds. . . . The wisest of all men had become the greatest of all fools for he had sinned against light and privilege and promise such that had been given to no man on the earth. . . . Truly, in Solomon we see how inferior the greatest human wisdom is to true piety. . . . Solomon's is the self-life having its full fling, and at the end turning away sad and sick of it all."

Accordingly, it is important to remember the lessons you learn early in life as you continue into your later years. In *Conformed to His Image: Biblical and Practical Approaches to Spiritual Formation,* Kenneth Boa exhorts:

"Our highest calling is to grow in our knowledge of Christ and make him known to others. If any person, possession, or position is elevated above the Lord Jesus in our minds or affections, we will be unable to fulfill this great calling. . . . A key secret of those who finish well is to focus more on loving Jesus than on avoiding sin. The more we love Jesus, the more we will learn to put our confidence in him alone."

Zooming **In**

For a man who ultimately surrounded himself with bad wives, Solomon certainly warned against it in his writings. In his proverbs, Solomon compared a bad wife to "decay in the bones," a quarrelsome wife to "constant dripping," a wayward wife to "a narrow well," and said that it was better to live in the desert or on the corner of the roof than to dwell with an argumentative wife.

Solomon was the second son of David and Bathsheba, whose relationship had begun amid adultery, murder, and death of their firstborn. Solomon had countless wisdom-increasing, teachable moments in his formative years, living in a home where his father increasingly put God first, even amid war, betrayal, and civic turmoil.

take a **CLOSER** look

> *Learn the lessons that God has prepared for you early in life, and keep what you have learned fresh in mind.*

Through the
Eyes of
Your Heart

Have you ever kept making the same mistake over and over again? What was it like to have to revisit the negative consequences of your errors?

_____

_____

_____

_____

Where in your life is it hard to obey God, despite the wisdom in doing so? What blessings can you imagine God will provide if you do obey?

_____

_____

_____

_____

Solomon did not finish well. What are some disciplines you can introduce into your life to help ensure that you do?

_____

_____

_____

_____

A Sheepish Discovery

This made the Pharisees and teachers of religious law complain that he was associating with such despicable people—even eating with them! So Jesus used this illustration: "If you had one hundred sheep, and one of them strayed away and was lost in the wilderness, wouldn't you leave the ninety-nine others to go and search for the lost one until you found it? And then you would joyfully carry it home on your shoulders."

Luke 15:2–5 NLT

The Big Picture

As Jesus traveled across the Israeli countryside, he rubbed shoulders with people who held permanent residence on the bottom rung of society's ladder. They were the unclean. They were the class of folks who were constantly stuck in sin. Whether it was the ceremonial laws of cleanliness that they never could fulfill or the legal statutes that they continued to break that made them unrighteous, they were the people who were always looking in from the outside of the Jewish temple.

Because of this, Jesus was constantly challenged by the legal experts and the spiritual authorities of his day. Jesus was a rabbi; he was a colleague of theirs, a respected teacher of God's truth. He even had a following of devoted students. For the Pharisees, this was problematic. They could not rationalize that someone who understood their law would willingly interact and walk among the population that they deemed to be untouchable.

They pressed their concern about his practices in the form of an accusation. In doing so, they removed any possibility or consideration that they might be in error. By laying the claim that "Jesus eats with sinners," they implied that Jesus was so disrespectful about the Old Testament law that he must be a heretic.

This put Jesus in a tough situation. He looked around and saw why they accused him. Dirty and diseased wretches, untrustworthy scoundrels, and desperate schemers living without hope surrounded him. They wanted to hear his message of God's love. They wanted to be touched by him in the new hope that a brush of his fingers might bring them healing. If indeed this was the accusation, then a simple scan of the crowd that wrapped around Jesus revealed that he was guilty.

As Jesus was inclined to do when the Pharisees challenged him, he answered their accusation with a series of parables. His stories enlightened the people who were seeking truth and confused those who were trying to stop him from meeting needs and bringing hope. He compared the people who made up his audience to a wandering sheep that would be hopelessly lost without the vigilant shepherd seeking it out regardless of distance or danger.

For more than two thousand years, the unworthy, unclean, and unimportant people of the world have celebrated these parables because they have identified themselves as the lost sheep and Jesus as the Shepherd, rejoicing in having been found and thankful that the Pharisees did not have the final word that day.

Amazing grace, how sweet the sound, that saved a wretch like me. I once was lost, but now am found; was blind but now I see.

John Newton

Take a Closer Look

A closer look at this parable reveals that God cares far more about making sure you are safe than he does about making sure you are good. Notice that Jesus never argues with the initial criticism that he spends his time with sinners and other unsavory people. Jesus makes no effort to defend the reputation of those around him.

Sheep were an important part of the culture of that day. They were vital to the economy and they were essential to religious expression. From a financial or religious standpoint, Christ's argument to go after a lost sheep made sense, particularly if the lost sheep was of good stock or physically unblemished. Jesus appealed to the universality of the inherent worth of the sheep. He argued rightly that they would all rejoice if such a creature of inherent value were rediscovered and made safe. How much more is this true when the creature that is lost is a person. Regardless of what led to the wandering and disconnection from the safety of the flock, Jesus declares that the inherent worth of a person is intrinsically valuable and precious and should incite rejoicing when brought safely into God's watch care.

> *The greatest form of praise is the sound of consecrated feet seeking out the lost and helpless.*
>
> Billy Graham

You may feel far from God right now for any number of reasons. Maybe you have never been to church, or maybe you simply haven't gone in years. Maybe you left to pursue other interests or were hurt. Maybe you have not prayed sincerely for some time. Maybe you have grown insensitive to the subtle grace of God around you. The good news is that God continues to seek you.

Apply It
to Your Life

God desires to keep you safe, and the best way for him to accomplish that is to keep you near him. He wants you to be secure in knowing he loves you, cares for you, provides for you, and protects you. He wants you to use the resources he offers through his Bible, his Spirit, his church, and his followers.

There may be people in this world who argue that you are not good enough, holy enough, smart enough, or successful enough to deserve God's blessings. The simple truth is that God's best blessing is experienced in safely belonging to him, and that all other blessings issue forth from this initial blessing. Jesus seeks you because he is "the Good Shepherd," and you matter to him.

God did not send his Son into the world to condemn its people. He sent him to save them!

John 3:17 CEV

From a cost-benefit consideration, Jesus' willingness to pursue one lost sheep and leave the other ninety-nine is an unthinkable risk, but completely in line with his character. Ben Witherington III wrote in *The New Testament Story*:

"This is a very peculiar shepherd indeed, but it is certainly true to the character and ministry of Jesus. He did see himself having as his mission seeking and saving the lost sheep of Israel. He did intentionally banquet with the bad and the wicked. Jesus viewed his ministry as a reclamation project in progress. This parable is however about seeking the lost."

Indeed, Jesus counts the costs and benefits using a completely different frame of thinking. The *Life Application New Testament Commentary* states:

"Jesus associated with sinners—people considered beyond hope—the Good News of God's Kingdom. . . . These tax collectors and sinners with whom Jesus associated were like lost sheep who had strayed away from God and needed to be returned. . . . In reality, the shepherds would not have had a party over one found sheep. Jesus used this element in his story to stress his kingdom's reality and the value of one lost person."

Zooming In

The imagery of a shepherd carrying home the lost sheep upon his shoulders paints the illustration of protection, rest, and provision. The once-lost sheep was safe atop the shepherd's shoulders, no longer in danger from predators. It did not have to expend any more effort in trying to forge its own trail, and it was in total submission to the confident direction of the shepherd.

Shepherds were a people of conflicted value in Jewish culture. In one regard, they were valued because they were the protectors of an essential commodity. As such, their expertise and skill were depended upon and begrudgingly respected. However, they were also disrespected because they were considered perpetually unclean since they worked with animals. As such, they were often excluded from religious ceremony and worship.

You can probably identify with finding something precious that was lost. God celebrates having you safely in his possession because he loves you.

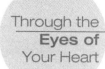

Through the
Eyes of
Your Heart

Have you ever found yourself alone and in a mess? What were the fears and feelings you had in that experience?

_____

_____

_____

What are some ways you feel safe in the hands of God while living in a world that is full of dangers?

_____

_____

_____

What are some ways you experience the joys of belonging to God that demonstrate his happiness of having found you?

_____

_____

_____

_____

Praying Right

When you pray, don't be like those show-offs who love to stand up and pray in the meeting places and on the street corners. They do this just to look good. I can assure you that they already have their reward. When you pray, go into a room alone and close the door. Pray to your Father in private. He knows what is done in private, and he will reward you. When you pray, don't talk on and on as people do who don't know God. They think God likes to hear long prayers. Don't be like them. Your Father knows what you need before you ask.

Matthew 6:5–8 CEV

The
Big Picture

Public prayer was common in the days of Jesus. In predominantly Jewish communities administrated by Roman authorities, religion was common, and offering prayers to a higher power was considered normal. In fact, praying in public often demonstrated that the person who prayed was religious and therefore honorable for business or social interaction. The Pharisees and scribes, who were the most learned and literate people of their culture in that day, often stood in public thoroughfares to offer long, articulate orations of prayer to affirm their righteousness and spiritual leadership over the common population. The better a man could speak in public, the more advantageous it was for him to do so in the context of prayer because he would be better respected and more highly regarded. This ability had little to do with actually communicating with God, but it had everything to do with succeeding in the religious culture that existed in Jesus' time.

It was in this environment that Jesus walked and performed miracles. In fact, Jesus was amazingly countercultural; he did not offer long, blustery commentary or petitions to God. He was a man of few words and dynamic action. When the citizens of regions compared who Jesus was and what he was doing with who the religious leaders were and what little they were doing, all their previous notions of powerful, effective prayer were turned upside down and inside out. Suddenly, the great words of the Pharisees seemed empty. The scribes' speeches were starkly shallow. They saw what Jesus was accomplishing, and they wanted to learn more.

Jesus understood this. When Jesus taught the crowds of people who were following him because they were amazed at the miracles he was performing, he deliberately included important instruction about talking with God in prayer. He shared what to pray, what not to pray, and also how to pray. Jesus taught that it is impossible to impress God with flowery speech and big words. God desires an economy of speech that expresses a sincere heart to connect with him. Prayer is not about choosing words that will amaze an audience; it is about a quiet, humble, and honest conversation with the God who created you and calls you to relate with him.

You need not cry very loud; He is nearer to us than we think.

Brother Lawrence

Take a
Closer Look

Two thousand years later, people still struggle with prayer. People today still think big words and complex sentences show how much they love God. Take a closer look at this passage to discover that prayer is much less about what you say than it is about how you say it.

When Jesus taught, he typically encouraged his audience and angered the Pharisees who opposed him. This time was no different. As Jesus instructed on prayer, every lesson took power and authority away from the enforcers of religion and placed it on the people who were now empowered to pursue a relationship with God.

Look at what Jesus taught them about prayer with these simple insights. Prayer did not have to be loud. It did not have to be long. It did not have to be complex. It did not have to be public. Jesus even went so far as to say that when prayer was overtly loud, long, complex, or prattling, it made a person look as though he did not know God at all. This assessment was a scathing indictment to the public prayer-givers and a strong encourage-ment to every person who des-perately wants to talk with God but sometimes cannot find the right words or any words at all.

God can pick sense out of a confused prayer.

Richard Sibbes

The teachings of Jesus on prayer can revolutionize your thinking about the time you spend with God. Jesus revealed that God already knows what you need before you ask, so prayer is not a procedural requirement to receive something from God's warehouse of spiritual supplies. God does not need you to give an educated speech or

well-developed religious essay, so prayer is not some award for a well-prepared oratory. In fact, Jesus said if that is your aim, as it was for the Pharisees, then you will get the reward of the acclaim of those who listen in, and little else. If you pray as though you do not know God by begging on, then you reveal that you really do not know much about the God of your prayers.

Your prayers should be simple expressions of love, of need, and of relationship to God. Ask him to forgive you for the mistakes you made. Keep this list short by going to him often. He knows what you did wrong, so just agree that your mistakes were wrong and ask him to help you do better next time, thanking him for his love, his mercy, and his kindness. Lay bare your needs, asking him to meet them out of his never-ending resources. Spend time with your heavenly Father. Listen more than you speak. Whether alone or in public, when you pray, have a private conversation with God.

The Holy Spirit helps us in our distress. For we don't even know what we should pray for, nor how we should pray. But the Holy Spirit prays for us with groanings that cannot be expressed in words. And the Father who knows all hearts knows what the Spirit is saying, for the Spirit pleads for us believers in harmony with God's own will.

Romans 8:26–27 NLT

How Others See It

Prayer blesses the prayer-giver as much as it allows a person to have communication with God. In his eponymous book *The Heart of George MacDonald,* author George MacDonald shares:

"Why pray, if God loves us and knows all we need before we pray? What if he knows prayer to be the thing we need first and most? What if the main object in God's idea of prayer be the supplying of our great, our endless need—the need of himself? . . . Communion with God is the one need of the soul beyond all other needs; prayer is the beginning of that communion."

Oswald Chambers, in *My Utmost for His Highest,* goes further:

"Prayer is the way to nourish one's life with God. Our ordinary views of prayer are not found in the New Testament. We look upon prayer as a means of getting things for ourselves; the Bible's idea of prayer is that we may get to know God Himself. It is not so true that 'prayer changes things' as that prayer changes me and I change things."

Zooming In

Orthodox Judaism historically allowed for individual prayer, and such practices were common until Israel was exiled by Babylon under King Nebuchadnezzar. The religious leaders emerging from the Exile determined that the scriptural knowledge of the common people was insufficient for individual prayer, so they created a book of orderly daily prayers called the *siddur*, which is used today by Jewish people across the world.

Oratory, or public speaking, was also an important part of Roman culture during the time of Jesus. Publicly spoken prayers by Romans identified the gods that a person followed and were given as part of community conversation to invite others into business transactions. Romans believed that if both sides of a transaction revered the same god, that god would honor their commerce. Business and religious expression were closely tied, with entire trade guilds established around these commonly followed gods.

The right way to pray involves personally communicating with God, no matter who shares your audience with him.

How would you describe your prayer practices? Do you find yourself trying to sound intelligent or spiritual when you pray in public? What are some things you could do to block out others when you pray publicly?

_____

_____

_____

Why do you think people speak unnaturally when they pray, such as speaking overly formally or repetitively? Do you talk to God the same way you talk to others? What are some things you do that are unnatural in your communication with God?

_____

_____

_____

How is it helpful to pray in private? What distractions come up when you pray in private? How can you overcome those distractions?

_____

_____

_____

_____

Altar-ing Worship

Noah went out, and his sons and his wife and his sons' wives with him. Every animal, every creeping thing, every bird, and whatever creeps on the earth, according to their families, went out of the ark. Then Noah built an altar to the LORD, and took of every clean animal and of every clean bird, and offered burnt offerings on the altar. And the LORD smelled a soothing aroma. Then the LORD said in His heart, "I will never again curse the ground for man's sake, although the imagination of man's heart is evil from his youth; nor will I again destroy every living thing as I have done."

Genesis 8:18–21 NKJV

The Big Picture

In the second month of the year, the rains started. For forty days, without a break, floodwaters fell from the sky and the springs of the deep burst forth. Five long months passed where all Noah and his family could see from the helm of the ark God had commanded the patriarch to build was a vast seascape of ocean. They probably did not even realize that the huge ark had come to rest atop a mountain peak until three months later, when the tops of the mountains became visible. Now this lone family knew the waters were receding. Yet four more months would pass before it was safe enough for the family and the menagerie they managed to emerge from the ark. All told, one year and ten days passed from the first raindrop to the time Noah set foot on dry land again.

The Bible does not record all that went through the minds of the only eight people on the earth. Their loneliness, sorrow, and fears were not captured

take a CLOSER look

for history's sympathy or analysis. Yet everything around them had been devastated, destroyed, and utterly washed away. Everyone who had mocked and ridiculed them for one hundred years was dead, forever buried by the global storm. But everyone who had ever shared a laugh with them rather than at them was also gone. Gone were all those whose chiding turned to crying as the waters rose and they beat on the sides of the ark, begging to be let in and saved from certain death. The parents and families of the wives of Noah's sons were all gone, lost forever.

Yet the Bible records that the first action Noah and his family took was to build an altar and to worship God upon it. They took some of the animals that the family had nurtured and protected through the storm and made a thanksgiving sacrifice to God. For one hundred years, Noah and his family had lived by their faith in God rather than by the ways of their people. That century of loneliness in a sea of disbelief was surpassed only by the one year of loneliness in a sea of solitude. When they emerged from the ark, they worshiped God because they realized that their Lord had led them through all those days to bring them to this day.

God seeks and values the gifts we bring Him—
gifts of praise, thanksgiving, service, and material
offerings. In all such giving at the altar we enter
into the highest experiences of fellowship.

G. C. Morgan

Take a
Closer Look

A closer look at Noah's first post-Flood worship experience reveals that true worship is the result of a relationship with the God who protects and provides, and not simply to fulfill religious law. When Noah and his family emerged from the ark, unharmed by their experience and ready to start anew, the law commanding sacrificial worship to God was still centuries away from being written. Yet it was the first action undertaken by this family.

Noah and his kin had every reason to worship God. First, God had kept the promise that he had voiced for one hundred years, that the rains would indeed fall. God also had kept his promise that Noah and his family would be protected through the rains, the floods, the death and devastation. God had also seen fit to have Noah and his family serve as the watch-keepers over all the types of animals of the earth, so that they, too, would escape the judgment of the Creator. God had also shown mercy to the ark's crew and cargo by bringing a rainbow and causing the waters to recede. Amid it all, they saw that God had remembered them. Accordingly, they worshiped—not because a law had mandated it, but because it was the most natural response of appreciation and adoration they could show to God.

> *I love Thee, dearest Lord, and in Thy praise will sing; solely because Thou art my God, and my most loving King.*
>
> Francis Xavier

Why do you go to church? Noah's example shows that the best reason to worship God is out of a heart that thanks God for all circumstances, good or bad. This is why God does not mandate worship, because he understands that to do so would only invite your worship to be empty and meaningless. Rather, while God commands you to

put him first, he simply encourages you not to forsake gathering with others to worship him. The logic in this is that when you put God first, you can see his fingerprints over all the details of your life. Accordingly, you will find cause to give him thanks for all the details of your life, whether you find the proverbial tide rising or falling.

The law cannot legislate love, requiring the fidelity and adoration of the one who gives it. If your worship is an expression of legal obligation rather than loving appreciation, it is really not worship at all, but a self-imposed spiritual penalty you pay that satisfies nothing. Each day, look around and take note of the provision and protection God offers you, and establish an altar of worship in your heart, thanking God for carrying you through the high, rough waters of life and for giving you a daily opportunity to start anew.

Willingly I will sacrifice to You; I will give thanks to Your name, O LORD, for it is good.

Psalm 54:6 NASB

How Others See It

Millie Stamm, in *He Is Real,* detailed the thankful heart of Noah after the ark's door dropped open and a new life awaited:

"What must Noah have felt as he looked at the devastation all around him? They had no food. They had no home. They would have to replenish the earth. What a gigantic undertaking! Where would they begin? Noah knew. There was no question in his mind. Noah had a close relationship with God. . . . As he realized anew what God had spared them from, his heart was filled with love and worship. The first thing he did was build an altar. There he offered a sacrifice of praise and worship to God."

Faith in God is expressed in heartfelt worship. Ronald Vallet, in *The Steward Living in Covenant,* explains how the faith of Noah in worshiping God after the Flood blessed every generation that followed:

"Noah built an altar and worshiped God with burnt offerings. God responded by covenanting with Noah, his descendants, and *every living creature* in a divine oath. God's covenant with Noah had a universal dimension: it was unconditional, unilateral, and everlasting. . . . Not only was it everlasting, it included all people. Because it was made apart from or before Israel, it is upheld apart from the community of faith, Israel. God's covenant with Noah made other covenants possible."

Zooming **In**

Cultural anthropologists have numbered between 250 and 300 accounts of flood stories from cultures around the world. These stories, some more mythic in detail than others, typically share details about a global flood, a single family being preserved, and a new chance for humanity emerging after the waters recede. Noah was protected from the Flood while the rest of humanity was not spared because the Bible says he "walked with God." This does not mean that Noah was without sin. Rather, it means that while he still had the capacity to offend God, he had a daily relationship with God that put God first. This assessment literally meant that Noah had no offense that God could attribute to him because Noah regularly sought God's forgiveness and favor through prayer.

God has promised to bless you as a descendant of Noah. Every rainbow is a reminder of that promise. Just as the rainbow is a reflection of God's goodness, so, too, should your worship reflect your love for him.

Through the
Eyes of
Your Heart

What de-motivates you to go to church? How is genuine worship bigger and more important than the obstacles that make church unappealing?

When you go to church, do you feel like you experience the presence of God, or are you just going through the motions? What blessings are you taking for granted that might help you reconnect with God this week in worship?

Noah built an altar as a physical reminder of where he had a significant encounter with God. What is the last "altar-ing" experience you had with God? What were the lessons you learned that still stay with you after that experience?

Risky Love

I am telling the truth in Christ, I am not lying, my conscience testifies with me in the Holy Spirit, that I have great sorrow and unceasing grief in my heart. For I could wish that I myself were accursed, separated from Christ for the sake of my brethren, my kinsmen according to the flesh.

Romans 9:1–3 NASB

The Big Picture

When the apostle Paul wrote the epistle to the church in Rome, he was not simply writing to another church seeking direction and leadership. Paul was writing to his friends and fellow citizens. Paul was a Roman citizen, a man with all the rights and privileges of any other resident of the world's leading city of the day. His deep love for the Roman people is reflected in his clear understanding of the numerous cultures that shaped the errant beliefs permeating Rome.

Paul was deeply troubled by the prideful religiosity of the Jewish population living in Rome and also by the deviant paganism held by the Gentile community there. Rome was the home of some of history's greatest minds, a repository for complex and progressive philosophical discussion. Yet it was also a cosmopolitan metropolis where every belief was allowed and every indulgence was tolerated. For Paul, the city of Rome presented great challenges and great opportunities.

The result of this challenging opportunity is the book of Romans, written to all the people of Rome regardless of what belief system they adopted or culture with which they affiliated. He was able to address his letter to the community in this manner because he knew that if his argument for Christianity could ever find an audience for consideration, it would be here where great minds fostered an atmosphere of great discussion. Because of this, Paul presented a classic treatise reasoning the case for following Jesus of Nazareth as the Messiah of God and the Christ for humanity.

In the first eight chapters of Romans, Paul establishes the doctrines of faith that serve as the basis for what he will teach about Jesus as God. The breadth and universal application of this good news for all people of Rome (and by extension, all of the world for today) are what has led some scholars to nickname this book "the gospel according to Paul." Whether Jew or Gentile, Roman national or foreign immigrant, God's judgment is upon all, and God's love is available to all through Jesus Christ. The final seven chapters launch from this platform by encouraging, exhorting, and compelling all people to therefore embrace God's love through faith in Christ so they can experience the judgment of praise and commendation rather than of punishment and condemnation.

In its totality, Paul's letter to the Romans is both an expertly crafted explanation of reasons why to live the Christian life, as well as a thorough instruction in how to do it.

Sacrifice is the only true measure of generosity.

Jason Hurst

If the book of Romans is understood as two parts linking the belief behind Christian living to the practice of living out those beliefs, a closer look at Romans 9:1–3 shows that the ultimate expression of a loving faith in action is selfless, sacrificial, dangerous, and costly. Despite its tremendous risk, it is also wonderfully rewarding.

Paul used every great tactic of a master logician. He argued historically and rationally. Yet, in these first verses of chapter 9, Paul moves from a sound argument to an impassioned plea. He would rather forsake heaven himself and accept the torment of eternity in hell, if it meant that his fellow Romans would embrace the gift of heaven.

This offer was no rhetorical tool. It no doubt would have shocked anyone who heard it and caused serious pause to anyone arguing against Christianity. It would have deflated any objection based on selfish motives or advancing a religious agenda, because Paul was willing to separate himself from the God for whom he pleaded, if his counterparts would in turn believe in Jesus as Lord. Paul showed that sharing faith in Jesus is not about winning an argument; it is about being willing to pay any cost, no matter how expensive, so that the other person can win the reward of heaven.

> *Give me love that leads the way, the faith that nothing can dismay, the hope no disappointments tire, the passion that will burn like fire. Let me not sink to be a clod; make me Thy fuel, Flame of God.*
>
> Amy Carmichael

Truly loving others is a risky proposition. Love often comes at great expense; it often entails giving up much so the person you love can gain much. For Paul, he was willing to give up his own promise of heaven if it meant his friends and fellow Romans could embrace those same promises offered by God. In this, it is impossible to separate real love from necessary sacrifice. Paul challenges you today to take the risk and pay the cost to experience the blessing of loving others sacrificially.

Whenever you assess the value of your personal relationships, it is worthwhile to count your personal cost for the potential of the other's gain. Any time you make the conscientious decision to love someone else sacrificially, doing so requires you to make withdrawals from your personal reserves of patience, trust, hope, and expectation. These personal withdrawals become deposits you invest with that other person. Wonderfully, in God's economy, your withdrawals are quickly replaced—from God's never-ending resources—with interest. The returns on your investment will inevitably pay eternal dividends. Just as Paul never had to worry about that which he was willing to forsake for his friends' benefit, neither do you need to risk losing the time, counsel, encouragement, and truth you invest in others in the name of love.

Greater love has no one than this, that he lay down his life for his friends.

John 15:13 NIV

How Others
See It

Paul's mind-set of sacrificial love should be the template that today's Christians copy in their own relationships with nonbelieving kin and fellow citizens. Ergun Caner wrote in *Christian Jihad: Two Former Muslims Look at the Crusades and Killing in the Name of Christ*:

"Paul's desire that he be 'cursed and cut off for the sake of my brothers' illustrates the unwavering compassion the apostle had for his Jewish kinsmen. . . . The gospel, first given to the Jews, will once again be accepted by many Jews at the consummation of the age. In the meantime, the duty of the Christian is to pray for the Jews, not to persecute them."

In *The Way of the Master,* Ray Comfort and Kirk Cameron offer a practical illustration:

"When an emergency vehicle drives through the city, the law demands that every other vehicle must pull over and stop. Why? Because someone's life may be in jeopardy. It is to be given great priority. That is how it should be when it comes to the eternal salvation of men and women. There is an extreme emergency. Everything else must come to a standstill or we are in danger of transgressing the Moral Law which demands, 'you shall love your neighbor as yourself.'"

Zooming **In**

The book of Romans not only presents a balanced view of the theology of the Christian life and the expression of it, it gives a strong encouragement to live a virtuous life because of the work of God. By weaving practical encouragements and rational points into his theological arguments, Paul reinforces that Christianity is more than something to just think about; Christianity is a life decision that shapes belief and conduct.

While it is unknown who originally took the gospel of Jesus to Rome, there were already a large number of Jewish synagogues there among the Roman population. Internal evidence in the book of Romans suggests that multiple Christian churches were meeting in Rome at the time of Paul's writing, hinting at early, widespread success in convincing both cultures that Jesus was indeed the Messiah for all people.

How have you benefited by this type of sacrificial love in your own relationships? Who has shown you this type of selfless love? How did they show you their love?

_____

_____

Paul was willing to give up heaven so that others might experience it. What spiritual blessings do you enjoy that you want to share with others? How will the lives of the people you care about be different if they receive what you possess by faith in God?

_____

_____

What would you put at risk by sharing your faith and loving others more sacrificially? What is the difference between risking your investments and investing your risks for the benefit of others?

_____

_____

You Complete We

It is right for me to feel this way about all of you, since I have you in my heart; for whether I am in chains or defending and confirming the gospel, all of you share in God's grace with me. God can testify how I long for all of you with the affection of Christ Jesus. And this is my prayer: that your love may abound more and more in knowledge and depth of insight, so that you may be able to discern what is best and may be pure and blameless until the day of Christ, filled with the fruit of righteousness that comes through Jesus Christ—to the glory and praise of God.

Philippians 1:7–11 NIV

The Big Picture

Roman prisons were severe. The accommodations were harsh, the treatment was cruel, and the company was dangerous. Typically, quarters were cramped, sunlight was rare, and disease was rampant. These prisons were often constructed below ground, usually next to cisterns. The prisons could have two levels, with the worst offenders being held in the lowest, dampest, darkest chambers, and lesser ones atop in the upper common area. Sometimes, high-profile prisoners were afforded more private quarters to ensure their safety until they could face judgment for their accused offenses.

Whatever the circumstance, the apostle Paul could have been focused on a lot of pressing considerations when he was jailed in Caesarea for two years awaiting trial before the Roman caesar, and he would have been forgiven for doing so.

However, he had his mind on more important matters. The Philippian church was facing a crisis, and they needed his help. They had a deep love for Paul, as he had both led in establishing the church and partnered with the church in other missionary efforts. Their affinity for one another had grown strong, and they had come to rely upon one another. Even though Paul was imperiled and imprisoned, when he received word that this dear congregation was struggling with some matters of doctrine, he decided to put his own calamities aside and reach out to them with guidance and direction.

It would be impossible for him to travel to them and help them sort out their messes. So, instead, he penned them a letter, knowing that it would be received with respect and deference. Again, Paul could have opened his missive to them complaining about his bad turn of events and griping about his horrible circumstances, but he instead chose to rejoice even in tough times. He opened with a positive message of the benefit of doing the right thing, no matter the risk, and thanked them for faithfully serving God with him across the miles, and in the face of constant opposition. This encouraging opening set the tone for the message he would deliver in the words to follow, and it reminded the burgeoning church that while it was important to deal with theological matters and doctrinal concerns, it was even more important always to celebrate the goodness of God in all situations.

May God, who gives this patience and encouragement, help you live in complete harmony with each other—each with the attitude of Christ Jesus toward the other.

Romans 15:5 NLT

**Take a
Closer Look**

While the book of Philippians has become known as a resource for understanding the way to true joy, a closer look at Philippians 1:7–11 reveals that the healthiest, most joyful relationships are found when both sides give 100 percent, rather than just going fifty-fifty.

The church in Philippi was known for its extremely generous nature. Elsewhere in the Bible, Paul commends the church for its financial help in supporting his mission efforts in starting a church in Jerusalem, even though the Philippian church was destitute and was not being asked to provide funds in any way. The church gave sacrificially and selflessly to Paul even at great expense to themselves because it believed in him and in the work he did.

Likewise, Paul gave freely of himself to the Philippian church even at a time of great inconvenience. He could not be with them, but he thought of them first and put their needs before his own. Doing so gave Paul tremendous joy because of the bond they shared in worshiping God, and helping them took his mind off his present troubles.

> *We are all in the same boat in a stormy sea, and we owe each other a terrible loyalty.*
>
> G. K. Chesterton

A popular but wrong-minded belief today is that relationships work when the partners give fifty-fifty. The reality is that if your relationships are going to succeed, both sides need to give 100 percent. Like Paul with the Philippians, you have to put others first in your relationships and trust that they will do the same. Only when you give all of yourself are your friends, family, and coworkers able to receive the fullness of blessing you have the potential to offer them.

Apply It
to Your Life

It is risky to be so vulnerable. The world encourages you to think about what you deserve out of your relationships, and to push for what you can gain. However, Paul's example shows that completely giving yourself to the needs of others—even when you yourself are in tremendous need—opens the door to a joyful understanding of the ways of God.

Paul tells the Philippian church that selflessly sharing in the grace of God by putting others first is necessary to a discerning mind, a depth of knowledge and insight, and a purity of living that honors God and fulfills you.

As the elect of God, holy and beloved, put on tender mercies, kindness, humility, meekness, longsuffering; bearing with one another, and forgiving one another, if anyone has a complaint against another; even as Christ forgave you, so you also must do. But above all these things put on love, which is the bond of perfection. And let the peace of God rule in your hearts, to which also you were called in one body; and be thankful.

Colossians 3:12–15 NKJV

In a world seemingly focused on celebrating the differences of people, God encourages his people to find unity in Christ so their differences can be used for a common purpose. In *The Handbook of Bible Application: New Living Translation* by the Livingstone Corporation, unity is the result of Christ's command to love each other:

"Have you ever longed to see a friend with whom you shared fond memories? Paul had such a longing to see the friends at Philippi. His love and affection for them was based . . . on the unity that comes when believers draw upon Christ's love. All Christians are part of God's family and thus share equally in the transforming power of his love."

In *The Church of Christ: A Biblical Ecclesiology for Today,* Everett Ferguson adds:

"The unity of Christ with the father is set forth as the image and goal of unity among believers. The gifts of Christ to his disciples are intended to achieve unity. The purpose stated for that unity is to bring the world to faith in Christ. . . . The fundamental experience of salvation in Christ argues against division. . . . Division is clearly branded as a sin."

Zooming **In**

Paul told the Philippians that it was "right" for him to think highly of his friends. More than that, though, the original language of his letter reveals that to remember the Philippian church in such a manner was also holy and righteous. When Christians think fondly of the friends with whom they share a common faith in Jesus, they are actually thinking the way God thinks.

Paul's favorable opinion of his friends exists whether he is under duress for sharing his faith or when he enjoys success and Christianity advances. Paul realized that when relationship is based on common faith rather than on selfish motives, the ups and downs of life are where the full range of a friendship is expressed, not proven.

Your spiritual relationships have been designed by God to be more than social contacts. They are the community that God has given you for a common purpose and mission, sharing belief and conviction.

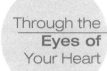

Through the
Eyes of
Your Heart

Who are your closest friends in your church or with whom you share a common faith? How would you describe those friends to others?

Who are fellow Christians or other church members that you do not think of so highly? Why is there a difference of opinion about those people? What can you determine to do to improve how you think of these potential friends?

How can you be a friend to other believers that you may have had problems with in the past? How can you experience unity even if you have little else in common? Commit to improving your Christian relationships so you both may enjoy the blessing.

Love Takes Time

Love is patient; love is kind. Love does not envy; is not boastful; is not conceited; does not act improperly; is not selfish; is not provoked; does not keep a record of wrongs; finds no joy in unrighteousness, but rejoices in the truth; bears all things, believes all things, hopes all things, endures all things.

1 Corinthians 13:4–7 HCSB

The Big Picture

First Corinthians 13 has become well known as the Love Chapter of the Bible. This famous chapter identifies the marks and expressions of real love. Perhaps the most interesting aspect of this chapter is that it is sandwiched between what may be the Bible's two most important chapters on orderly worship. As the apostle Paul wrote to the emerging church in Corinth, he offered them admonition and instruction designed to help the church get on track and stay focused. Part of Paul's cautionary leadership detailed what should or should not be included in the times when the group of believers gathered together to worship God corporately. In the apex of this instruction, Paul takes a literary pause and exhorts them not to forget about love.

Paul's inclusion of "Love 101" is vital because by inserting this chapter in the middle of teaching them about worship, he highlights the reality that worship, without love, is pointless. If the church were to be ignorant or dismissive about love, then all they could say about themselves was that they were yet another religious system. Without love, they would be only another group of struggling, futile people, vainly and ineffectively trying to reach God.

However, by remembering love, they could accomplish so much more, because God himself is the definition, description, and originator of love. By conscientiously integrating love into and distributing love out of their worship, they would be re-creating that which God is, and they would be worshiping within the context from which they themselves were created.

Because of love, the church was far different and so much more than just another religion. Because of love and orderly worship expressed through love, they would have communion with God. They would offer prayers and songs of praise and thanksgiving. The church leaders would share encouraging words of truth. They would explore the scrolled Scriptures together. They would dine together, laugh together, learn together, and love together. They would experience the reality of God in their lives, and their worship would be a real encounter with the living God, rather than a ritualistic offering to a distant, unknowing, unknowable deity. As they worshiped God and grew in their understanding of love and its expressions, they would apply those lessons to their relationships with other people, and the world would never be the same because of it.

A friend loves at all times, and a brother is born for a difficult time.

Proverbs 17:17 HCSB

**Take a
Closer Look**

However tempting it may be to examine 1 Corinthians 13 as the ingredients of love, a closer look at this famous passage shows that love is not simply a recipe of components combined together; it is a spiritual confection that requires time to cook to perfection.

According to this passage, every expression of love requires one common factor—time. You cannot be patient with someone without time. In fact, if you do not make the time, you are proving to be impatient, and therefore unloving. As you go through the ingredients of love, you discover that to truly feel or express those aspects of love, you have to either spend time with that person, invest time in that person, or take time to forget about your self in deference to the one you love.

People do not fall in love nearly so much as they grow in love because of time spent together. The more time you give to another, focusing on that person, the more you find lovable about that person, the more you are willing to forgive, and the more you are willing to give for the relationship.

> *Time is too slow for those who wait, too swift for those who fear, too long for those who grieve, too short for those who rejoice, but for those who love, time is eternity.*
>
> Henry Van Dyke

As you evaluate your relationships, you may be able to make a connection between troubles that you have and the lack of time you are spending with the other person. If you cannot seem to connect with your child, your spouse, or even a friend, spend more time with that person.

The more you are with someone, the more you will understand that person. You will understand why your friend always cries during romantic movies, you will eventually see why your mate is insecure around coworkers, or why your child likes reading poetry rather than fiction. You may not agree with any of them, but you will grow closer to the ones you love the more time you spend with them.

Spending time with loved ones also makes you more compassionate in your dealings with them. You are able to move beyond those little differences or habits that used to annoy you, and you know their idiosyncrasies are part of the person you love. As you spend more time, sharing more experiences with them, the more you are able to walk through difficult times with them and share the peaks and valleys of life together.

True love rarely happens at first sight, and deep love never does. The path to abiding love is a scenic route that takes time to travel before reaching the destination.

Friend, you have no idea how good your love makes me feel, doubly so when I see your hospitality to fellow believers.

Philemon 1:7 MSG

Sometimes biblical love is not very romantic, but the lasting result from gritty, determined love is enduring and significant. As shared in the Zondervan book *Creative Bible Lessons in 1 & 2 Corinthians: 12 Lessons about Making Tough Choices in Tough Times*:

"On second thought, forget the candles, put the roses away, and turn off the CD, because the love we are talking about has very little to do with romance. No Hallmark sentiments here—we are talking about the kind of love that demands hard work, sacrifice, and vulnerability. It is not the kind of love you feel; it is the kind you do. The kind of love Jesus modeled."

David A. Stoop and Stephen Arterburn add in *The Life Recovery Bible*:

"Most of us define love as an emotion and stop there. But in 1 Corinthians 13:4–7, Paul defined love as a commitment to act a certain way toward others. We may not always be able to conjure up the feelings and emotions of love, but we can certainly choose to practice the behaviors he listed in these verses. The apostle knew that when we behave in loving ways, feelings of love soon follow."

Zooming **In**

One expression of true love explained in this passage is that it endures all offenses and is long-suffering. The terminology for "endures all things" in the Greek language comes from a root word that literally means "roofs over." The word picture shows an offended person who actually builds a roof to protect an offender, rather than expelling him or her due to the offense.

Several of the expressions of love are explained negatively ("is not boastful," "does not envy"). By doing this, Paul tapped into the commonly understood manner in which love was expressed in his day, but in reality was selfish lust or infatuation. Paul was giving the believers in Corinth a clear choice between the true love that comes from faith in God and the shallow impersonation of love offered by the world.

In the choice between quantity time and quality time with those you love, choose both.

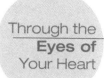
Through the
Eyes of
Your Heart

Even if love at first sight is possible, what is it about spending more time with those you love that helps you love those people even more?

How have the trials and difficulties you have experienced with loved ones helped you experience a deeper, more mature love relationship?

In what ways does an active, loving relationship help you to be a less envious, more patient person? How does your love for others strengthen them in similar ways?

Open Water

He said, "Come!" And Peter got out of the boat, and walked on the water and came toward Jesus. But seeing the wind, he became frightened, and beginning to sink, he cried out, "Lord, save me!" Immediately Jesus stretched out His hand and took hold of him, and said to him," You of little faith, why did you doubt?"

Matthew 14:29–31 NASB

The Big Picture

The story has captured the imaginations of generations and given hope for the common person to accomplish the miraculous: Peter, the impetuous follower of Jesus, driven by faith and compelled by love, takes a step from the wooden fishing boat onto the glassy wet surface of the Sea of Galilee. Amazingly, Peter's trembling foot neither breaks the thin liquid pane nor submerges under the weight of his step. As though his entire body were a leaf resting atop the water's face, Peter defied natural law and common thought and stood atop the Sea of Galilee, just a few short steps away from Jesus of Nazareth.

In this day filled with miracles where the twelve apostles saw Jesus heal an untold number of sick and hurting people, then later witnessed him turn two fish and five loaves of bread into a feast to feed a multitude, this latest feat left them most awed and amazed. After feeding the crowd, Jesus had excused himself to pray, as he often did. Prayer was no ritual for their leader; it seemed to strengthen and empower him. It was a dominant part of his

take a CLOSER look

daily routine, but his prayer was never routine. Now, as they had cast off the shores of the Galilean sea without him as he prayed, they found him walking out to them to catch up to the boat.

Peter cast his eyes upon Jesus as he approached and implored his Master to call him out. For a few shaky steps, the apostle walked a watery path that no one has ever literally followed. Only when Peter took his eyes off Jesus did everything collapse beneath his feet. Looking around, Peter realized the wind was whipping around him, possibly splashing water against his legs. Suddenly, his brain could not logically process the phenomenon that he experienced. When his brain could not make sense of the miraculous, fear swooped in. Instantly, Peter buckled beneath the water, and he was immediately in need of a lifeguard.

Throughout the generations to follow, people read of Peter's faith and were similarly moved even though his trek was brief and ended in being rescued. Because Peter left the safety of the boat., he inspired innumerable others to follow upon their own walks of faith down paths that seemed impossible or illogical, just to be closer to Jesus.

Then Jesus said to the disciples, "Have faith in God."

Mark 11:22 NLT

Take a
Closer Look

While it is appropriate to celebrate Peter's victory because he stepped out in faith when logic told him to stay on board the boat, a closer look highlights the encouraging truth that Jesus responded immediately to Peter's desperate cry, saving the terrified follower.

As soon as Peter crashed through the sea's surface, Jesus extended an arm to save him. Jesus did not allow him to thrash and flail in the cold black water of night. He did not pause or even wait to teach the apostle a lesson about staying focused and trusting obediently. Without hesitation, Jesus (who himself still stood safely upon the water) reached down and lifted his friend to safety.

What an intense, unforgettable journey for Peter, to go from taking strides of faith that defied every human comprehension to falling dramatically into the chilling, relentless waves of the Sea of Galilee, only to be lovingly and instantly pulled into a secure embrace by his Lord. While the lesson of walking by faith and not by sight would reverberate through history, surely the security of being instantly rescued by Jesus is what empowered Peter to take further steps of impossible greatness throughout the rest of his life.

> *Faith never knows where it is being led, but it loves and knows the One who is leading.*
>
> Oswald Chambers

The experiences you process through your five senses rarely align with faith experiences. If they did, there would be no need for faith, which is nothing less than a total reliance upon God for the provision of any given situation. Any time you find yourself taking a faith step, you will likely find yourself soon thereafter having a crisis of belief because of the inevitable conflict that occurs when faith meets everyday living.

Apply It
to Your Life

Perhaps you took a step out even when it did not make sense. Maybe you took a new job, or left a good job. Maybe you relocated, or got involved in a new ministry at church. Not long after a few victorious strides where you experienced blessing, you looked around to see the world crashing in. Bills piling, overwhelming demands on your time, or friends and family pressuring you. Before you knew it, the blessing had passed and you were sinking . . . fast.

In those panicked or scary moments of life, take comfort in knowing that Jesus is ever present. As he did with Peter, Jesus offers a hand up to you, ready to rescue you with a warm embrace. He will not make you flounder just to prove a point. He is the guardian of your life; and he is only a heart's cry away.

The simple truth is that if you had a mere kernel of faith, a poppy seed, say, you would tell this mountain, "Move!" and it would move. There is nothing you wouldn't be able to tackle.

Matthew 17:20 MSG

Jesus had a habit of immediately coming to the rescue of those in need. He can be trusted to do the same today; it is his nature to do so. Frederick Dale Bruner writes in *Matthew: A Commentary*:

"Jesus 'immediately' extending a hand to rescue Peter reminds us of his quick response to the leper and the centurion. Believers learn from the gospel that whenever they are in need and come to Jesus, he is 'immediately' there with strong hands to help. Nevertheless, Jesus scolded Peter. 'O you man of little faith! Why did you doubt?' Fortunately, Jesus saves before he scolds."

Christ's scolding is not a condemnation, but an encouragement to trust him. In *If You Want to Walk on Water, You've Got to Get Out of the Boat*, John Ortberg writes:

"Jesus is still looking for people who will dare to trust him. He is still looking for people who will refuse to let fear have the last word or to be deterred by failure. He is still looking for people who will respond to his call and step out of the boat."

Zooming **In**

The Sea of Galilee is not a sea at all, but in reality the lowest freshwater lake in the world. The Bible also refers to the body of water as the Sea of Gennesaret. Due to the lake's surrounding geography, it is well known for its windy waterscape and sudden, often violent storms.

This famous lake is the setting for many important biblical events. In addition to Peter's dramatic water walk, the Sea of Galilee was also where Jesus calmed the storm, taught the Sermon on the Mount, and fed 5,000 hungry followers with five loaves of bread and two fish. Also, its shores were the workplace of the fishers Peter, Andrew, James, and John, the apostles called to follow Jesus.

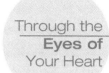
Sometimes, taking a giant risk does not result in giant victory. Even in those times when you need God to rescue you, take courage in knowing that he is there for you, ready to help you at a moment's notice.

Have you ever taken a risk for God? If so, what was the experience and how did it turn out? To what do you attribute the success or failure of your experience?

Have you ever cried out to God to help you? How can you see that God met your needs? Do you think you cried out because you took your eyes off God or allowed your faith to weaken because of the circumstances?

Knowing that God is eager to support or even rescue should encourage you to do great things for God. How are risks less frightening or imposing knowing that God is able to immediately help? Does God's promise give you a more courageous faith?

On-the-Job Resources

Most assuredly, I say to you, he who believes in Me, the works that I do he will do also; and greater works than these he will do, because I go to My Father. And whatever you ask in My name, that I will do, that the Father may be glorified in the Son. If you ask anything in My name, I will do it.

John 14:12–14 NKJV

The Big Picture

The hour was late. A betrayal had been scheduled, and Jesus would be faithful to keep the appointment. All around him, the eleven remaining apostles listened somberly as Jesus shared a final message of encouragement and assignment. In the context of the news that Jesus would soon be leaving them, these weary followers were being commissioned to change the world.

In their remaining time together, Jesus would tell his followers that they would be responsible for taking the message of God's redeeming love to the entire world. They would be pressed into humiliating service, similar to what he had modeled in washing their muck-covered feet. The night's meal had begun with certain members of the group of followers arguing over which of them was the greatest; now Jesus was telling them that they had been prepared for a mission and that they would likely die in obscurity.

Jesus pulled no punches in telling what awaited them. He had already revealed that Judas was a betrayer, and plainly stated that despite his best intentions, Peter would soon deny being a follower of Jesus. To all who remained, he told them that they would follow where he was soon going, telling them in language they well understood that to be a follower of Christ meant a likely death for such allegiance.

However, Jesus also gave encouragement and hope along with the difficult facts. He told them that they would not be alone; they would receive guidance from God's Holy Spirit. He also affirmed that God would go before them to prepare the hearts of those with whom they would be sharing. As if it were not overwhelming enough to try to comprehend the preparatory and indwelling work of God in each of their lives, the apostles then sat amazed as Jesus promised them that they would accomplish even greater things than he had.

Jesus was the one who had turned water into wine. He had fed a multitude out of a meager meal. He had cured the lepers, brought sight to the visionless, and even raised the dead. He had confronted demoniacs and religious hypocrites. He had brought hearing to the deaf, speech to the mute, and footsteps to the lame. Now Jesus was promising that they would do greater things still.

Little did they know that they would be the ones from whom the world would discover the hope God offers through faith in Jesus. They had no way of knowing the generations of people whose lives would be changed. They could not yet know, because that night in the Upper Room, all was still just a promise.

You cannot climb the ladder of success dressed in the costume of failure.

Zig Ziglar

Most attention on this passage is given to a traditional reading that focuses on how a right-minded person can do awesome feats. A closer look shows that this is not really the case; in reality, what Jesus promised the apostles was that what they asked for in his name would be the work that Jesus himself did through them, for the acclaim of God.

Biblical history records that the apostles accomplished many great works, performing miracles of healing while sharing the gospel of faith in Jesus as Lord. They managed to challenge the beliefs of many and to rile the administrations of many countries. They worked and spoke with such authority and effectiveness that they quickly developed religious opposition everywhere they went. And without fail, all the apostles eventually died as martyrs for their faith.

A review of the apostles' accomplishments shows that it was Jesus who worked through his followers. They did work and accomplished feats that are not humanly explainable. They were all simple, uneducated people who had no standing, privilege, or influence, yet they literally changed the world around them. The key was that back in the Upper Room, on the night that Jesus was betrayed, he had shown them that they must abandon their own motives for God's and allow his agenda to determine everything they did afterward.

> *That some achieve great success, is proof to all that others can achieve it as well.*
>
> Abraham Lincoln

When a person is submitted to God, Christ produces. Being submitted means serving God no
matter the cost. As the apostles discovered, submission is the key to the greatest experiences you
will ever have in your life. When you put yourself
at the top of your planning chart, your experiences and opportunities will likely be quite limited

and fairly provincial. However, by relinquishing yourself to the will of God to
know him and to make him known to others, the doors to the entire world
open wide.

The chances are more likely than not that you will never touch someone
and see him or her healed from a sickness or disease. You probably will
never give sight to the blind or raise a crippled person to walk. However, God
has given you the greatest ability of all, to share his eternal life-giving message to a world that is desperate for hope. You can share with anybody who
will listen. You can advance God's agenda by turning your own agenda over
to him. Of all the great things you could possibly do, being on God's team
offers the greatest potential.

*May He grant you your heart's desire
and fulfill all your counsel!*

Psalm 20:4 NASB

Jesus promised that his followers not only would do great things, but that they would do even greater things than he. What limits people today from such experience appears to be a lack of belief in the promise. Dr. David Stevens wrote in *Jesus, M.D.: A Doctor Examines the Great Physician*:

"If Jesus really expects us to do 'even greater things' than he did, then why do not we see a lot more impossible things being done today? Why do not we see more of the Great Physician's followers specialize in impossible cases? . . . We seem to have forgotten . . . what the Great Physician told his interns just a short time after he raised Lazarus."

Lynda Hunter Bjorklund reveals that the Bible's Philip (whose question prompted Jesus' promise) struggled with the same problem that inhibits many people today. In *The Hungry Heart: Satisfy Your Desire to Know God in Deeper Ways*, she wrote:

"Philip must have thought to himself, *Greater things than Jesus did? Healing? Casting out demons? Raising the dead? How can this be?* Philip lived beneath what Jesus desired for him. He had low expectations and had become satisfied with a so-so life. He reduced the 'greater things' to what people could see with their own eyes. . . . Jesus said he would reveal himself to those who believe in him. In other words, Jesus would allow those who believe in him to 'know' him."

Zooming **In**

Jesus promised "most assuredly" that the disciples would do greater works than he. The word translated "most assuredly" is the historic *verily* and derives from the Hebrew word for amen, the common ending to prayers. *Amen* is Hebrew's strongest, most reliable affirmation, possibly why the word has never been translated from the original language. It means that whatever statements were spoken in context with the "amen" were reality. For Jesus to exhort his promise with this "amen" was to encourage the listeners that his claim was far more than a pep rally; it was a guaranteed reality they could expect to happen.

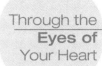
Every day, followers of Christ experience the miracu-lous every time they share their faith or do acts of kindness in Christ's name. You, too, can see these wonders in your own life if you trust God to use you.

What are some things you have done for others because you believed God wanted you to do them? What were the results?

Any time a person experiences the love and truth of God through any person, God has performed a miracle. What are some miracles you have been a part of, either as a giver or a receiver?

God has promised that anything you ask for in the name of Jesus, you will receive. What spiritual blessing, encouragement, or boldness have you ever received because of asking for it in prayer? How can you use that spiritual resource in Christian service now?

Hide-and-Seek

Turn to the LORD! He can still be found. Call out to God! He is near. Give up your crooked ways and your evil thoughts. Return to the LORD our God. He will be merciful and forgive your sins. The LORD says: "My thoughts and my ways are not like yours. Just as the heavens are higher than the earth, my thoughts and my ways are higher than yours. Rain and snow fall from the sky. But they don't return without watering the earth that produces seeds to plant and grain to eat. That is how it is with my words. They don't return to me without doing everything I send them to do."

Isaiah 55:6–11 CEV

The Big Picture

The prophet Isaiah spoke to Israel during the time of world history when the nation was divided and under the rule of foreign invaders. He served as the mouthpiece for God for more than forty years, speaking forcefully and faithfully, foretelling future events and even prophesying about the Messiah who would be the Savior of all humanity.

These prophecies about the Messiah tended to consume Isaiah's public speaking late in his life. These foreshadowing exclamations gave hints of everything about the Messiah's name, his lineage, his appearance, his conduct, his exploits, his purpose, and his effectiveness. Most of these prophecies could not be understood fully without the context of history, but even in speaking them to the people of Israel at God's command, Isaiah gave the populace great hope and expectation. The religious community captured his messianic prophecies with excitement and honed their search for the political deliverer God had promised to them, even as they bristled at Isaiah's

take a CLOSER look

accompanying prophecies that called the nation to reject its inappropriate ways and spiritual compromise.

Even while Isaiah prophesied, world history played out all around them. During his tenure, Isaiah witnessed Israel to the north submissively align with the Assyrians and saw the northern city of Samaria destroyed. Isaiah saw his own king Hezekiah follow his advice to resist the Assyrians—even at great risk—which in turn caused the mighty invaders to again attack the Northern Kingdom. This time, however, Assyria fell to unexpected defeat, Hezekiah finished his reign peacefully, and Isaiah's prophecies ended.

Isaiah was driven by a consuming, uncompromising view of God that exalted the Lord as pure and holy. The prophet's perception of himself was radically altered when his understanding of God was changed from what he had been trained to think about him to what he experienced firsthand. That tension between Israel's historic, pervasive understanding of God and Isaiah's comprehensive, righteous view would serve as both the source and idiom of the prophet's messages throughout his life. Isaiah understood God to be mighty enough to protect his own nation of people even against the mightiest of foes, yet personal enough to be concerned over the affairs of individuals. Between their struggles in the present and their faith-filled remembrances of the past, they looked to the days ahead with a limited understanding of when their land would be their own, and they could autonomously live in the fulfilled promises delivered through a Messiah.

God never gives us information about himself merely to satisfy our curiosity. All that we need to know about him is this life he has told us.

Robert Crossley

The prophet Isaiah offers hope and promise that God desires to be found. Most common readings focus on how difficult it is to know God's thoughts because they are so different from the thoughts of people. A closer look, however, reveals that in order to see God as he truly is, searchers must be willing to abandon their preconceived notions of him in light of his truth.

Israel had long been known for its stubbornness and rebelliousness. Prophets spoke out again and again for Israel to recognize God for who he is, rather than for who the nation wanted him to be. Isaiah offered the promise that God wanted to be understood accurately, because in this, they could experience the full earthly blessings provided by him, blessings that could protect them. However, they filtered his declarations through their own expectations, through their own understanding, and through their own strategies of survival in the warring world around them.

God promised Israel that their trust in God would return dividends that they had not experienced in generations. If they would close their eyes to the overwhelming circumstances around them, and open their minds to the potential that God was greater than they had imagined, the blessings would be incredible.

> *What matters supremely, therefore, is not, in the last analysis, the fact that I know God, but the larger fact which underlies it—the fact that He knows me.*
>
> J. I. Packer

Many different people hold various opinions about God. Some view him as an unknowable force of energy, while others view him as a cosmic time-keeper of the universe who is distant from the earth and the people on it. Even within Christianity, many people show with their conduct that what they believe about God is different from what they actually say they believe.

It is good news that God wants you to know who he is and how he operates. He wants to show you that his power, his resources, and his love are all available to you. God wants you to know this so that your perception of him will come into alignment with the reality of who he is, and that your new understanding of God will radically change your relationship with him. God wants you to come to him and trust him for all your needs, rather than trusting in others, or even trusting in yourself. If you forsake your preconceived notions about God and trust him according to how he himself says he his, your life will be better than anything you could have imagined on your own.

It is just as the Scriptures say, "What God has planned for people who love him is more than eyes have seen or ears have heard. It has never even entered our minds!"

1 Corinthians 2:9 CEV

How Others
See It

Isaiah 55 reveals the effectiveness in the Word of God. This reliability was pronounced to Israel by the prophet. The written record of that pronouncement encourages believers today with the same unchanging truth. In *The Power of a Positive Woman,* Karol Ladd wrote:

"Remember, God sees the whole picture from a heavenly viewpoint; we only see the narrow situation right before our eyes. Isaiah 55:8–9 reminds us of God's eternal perspective and our own lack of sight. . . . These faith-building words help us realize that we do not understanding everything—but God does. . . . God understands our situation much better than we do. We are probably not the best ones to be calling the shots.

Zooming In

Isaiah's prophecies both encouraged and convicted the people of Israel. In many of the pronouncements voiced by the prophets, the enemies of Israel were told to expect defeat as they opposed God. However, Judah itself was exhorted not to take its covenant with God for granted. The continuing sin and idolatry of Judah's people put them at risk of completely breaking the covenant and making them vulnerable to the attacks of their enemies.

While God's thoughts cannot be comprehended, your faith in him can be apprehended. Grab hold of trusting God, and embrace the adventure that will exceed your every expectation.

The nearness of God promised to Israel through the prophet Isaiah communicated more than just his location. God was near in the concept of time—he would respond to their needs instantly. Furthermore, God was near to them relationally—he would protect them the way a mother hen protects her brood or a father defends his family.

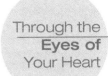
God is bigger than your biggest thought and is certainly not limited by your limitations. Expand your faith by expanding your belief in God.

What are some issues that you thought were too big for God? What issues have you thought were too small or unimportant? How does your opinion of God change when you know that he wants you to share all your burdens with him?

_____

_____

God's thoughts are higher than your thoughts. What does this mean to you? How can you use this truth as an encouragement for the struggles you face?

_____

_____

_____

God's words always accomplish what they are spoken to do. What is an example where you have seen failure despite your best effort (either in words or deeds)? How will you turn your needs over to God in the future?

_____

_____

_____

What a Catch!

Then Jonah prayed to his God from the belly of the fish. He prayed: "In deep trouble, I prayed to God. He answered me. From the belly of the grave I cried, "Help!" You heard my cry. You threw me into ocean's depths, into a watery grave, with ocean waves, ocean breakers crashing over me. I said, "I've been thrown away, thrown out, out of your sight. I'll never again lay eyes on your Holy Temple." Ocean gripped me by the throat. The ancient Abyss grabbed me and held tight. My head was all tangled in seaweed at the bottom of the sea where the mountains take root. I was as far down as a body can go, and the gates were slamming shut behind me forever—Yet you pulled me up from that grave alive, O God, my God!

Jonah 2:1–6 MSG

The Big Picture

The opening of the Bible's book of Jonah shares everything you need to know about how the predicament that Jonah found himself in came to pass. God told the prophet to go to Nineveh and Jonah disobeyed.

Jonah had plenty of reasons to decline the opportunity. The people were wicked. They worshiped false gods and engaged in unspeakable acts as part of their worship. They were a violent people who had won many battles in establishing the reputation for Nineveh as a great city. The people of Nineveh were also well to do, as the city was a major hub of commerce upon the Tigris River. If ever there appeared to be an opportunity for failure, it was the prospect of traveling far away to this mighty city belonging to the Assyrians and telling its citizens that they must turn away from their ungodly habits or receive punitive judgment from God.

While all of this could have implicated Jonah's thinking, his true motives for disobeying are made clear later in the book; he did not want to give the Ninevites

God's message because if they heard it, they would likely believe in it. The only thing that was more unpalatable to Jonah about actually going to this pagan land and speaking God's message to his enemies was the prospect that he would actually be effective and that the Assyrians would escape the wrath of God.

The Bible details Jonah's attempt to outrun God. Rather than passively disobey and just stay put at home, Jonah actively disobeyed and decided to travel in the other direction. God literally told the prophet to go northeast, so Jonah determined to travel southwest. By Jonah's reasoning, if it took him three years to arrive at his destination because of his self-imposed exile upon an opposite-heading ship, then perhaps he could outwait God or outlast Nineveh. To him, either prospect was more appealing and less risky than actually obeying.

Jonah discovered the hard way not to test God's resolve. God used a catastrophic storm, a ship full of terror-ridden sailors, and a very big fish to keep his plan on track. The giant fish swallowed Jonah whole soon after the sailors had thrown him overboard, in a desperate attempt to calm the seas and save their own lives. For three days Jonah languished in the fish's innards, wrapped in seaweed and contemplating the foolishness of his own rebellion.

Then, the fish beached itself and vomited Jonah upon the shore. God was there, waiting for the prophet with his original command to go to Nineveh. God showed that he was committed to giving the Ninevites another chance, and he was committed to giving them that chance through Jonah.

A soul that is reluctant to share does not as a rule have much of its own. Miserliness is here a symptom of meagerness.

Eric Hoffer

Jonah's story is the Bible's biggest fish tale. However, a sincere examination of this important passage shows how Jonah learned firsthand that God will go to extraordinary lengths to restore a person to fulfill the plan God has established.

Jonah's experiences demonstrate that God's plan will not go unfulfilled. Try as he might, Jonah could not escape the plan of God. Jonah discovered that every person, every living thing, and every created thing in the universe is under the control of God. Accordingly, he will put anything and everything into his employ to work out his good and perfect plan through those whom he calls to serve.

Jonah loved God. He just did not love the Ninevites. In using Jonah to extend the message of a second chance to Nineveh, God implemented a plan that would teach both the rebellious nation and the defiant prophet the persistent, consistent love of God. Jonah would ultimately relent and take God's message to the rebellious nation of 120,000 people in need of another opportunity. Today, Jonah's story honors the persistent love that God has even for the most wayward people, whether they call themselves his friends or enemies.

Genius is perseverance in disguise.

Mike Newlin

God is calling. He has a specific plan for you. It may be big and dramatic, taking you across the world. It may be small and ordinary, taking you across the street. Whether he wants you to go around the corner or around the globe, what matters is whether or not you agree to go.

Apply It
to Your Life

God is exceedingly patient and amazingly kind. No reports of passenger-carrying whales have hit the news lately, but people testify all over the world about how God waited them out, changed their circumstances, or put subtle (or not-so-subtle) reminders in their lives that his plans await fulfillment.

Maybe you put God on hold while you started your career. Perhaps you decided that you could put your spiritual plans on the back burner while you gave your immediate attention to your family, your health, or even your happiness. Maybe you, like Jonah, ran in the opposite direction from God because you did not like where he was telling you to go or what he was telling you to do. Yet, in the quiet of your heart, you know that the opportunity to obey is still open. God is calling. The time has come to answer.

To those who by persistence in doing good seek glory, honor and immortality, he will give eternal life.

Romans 2:7 NIV

Not only was Jonah's life an illustration of the futility of trying to outmaneuver God, he was also an example of effective prayer. Tom Carter detailed Jonah's prayer habits in *They Knew How to Pray: 15 Secrets from the Prayer Lives of Bible Heroes*:

"Sometimes God helps us, not by taking us out of the crisis, but by taking the crisis out of us. That was true of Jonah, because while he was still in the fish's stomach, he testified to the Lord, 'You listened to my cry' (Jonah 2:2). God was helping him, not by taking him out of his problem, but by being with him in his problem."

The full answer to prayer combines God's provision with a fresh opportunity to obey his commands. In *All the Prayers of the Bible,* Herbert Lockyer wrote:

"The sea was God's sea and Jonah was God's prophet, and a prayer stool was found in the heart of the raging waters. Prayer was answered and with a renewed consecration and commission Jonah arose and went to Nineveh. How grateful we should be that in our deepest trouble we can pour out our heart before the Lord and experience his power to deliver us from the sea of distress."

Zooming **In**

The name Jonah derives from the Hebrew word meaning "dove." In the book of Genesis, when the global floodwaters receded, Noah sent out a dove, and the bird returned with an olive branch as a signal of hope. Similarly, the prophet Jonah went to Nineveh with a message of hope to a people who would otherwise be subject to God's judgment.

Although Nineveh initially repented, they ultimately did not embrace God's offer given through Jonah. Despite God's faith-fulness in blessing Nineveh for turning away from their past practices, the warring community eventually returned to their unholy habits. Consequently, their hub of commerce eventually was overtaken first by the Medes, then later by the Babylonians. Thought by scholars to be the largest city in the world in 688 BC, it was completely leveled by enemies in 612 BC, and its citizens either escaped, were slaughtered, or were deported as slaves.

You cannot outrun, outlast, outwit, or outthink God. Rather than hide from him or defy him, agree that his plan for you is best and discover the adventure he has prepared.

Do you have a Nineveh of your own? Is there a place you just do not want to go, even if God were leading you to go there? What is it about that place that makes it so undesirable?

_____

_____

Imagine that place being different because God used you to make a difference. Do you believe God can use you? Maybe that place is a family relationship or even your own work. What problems with the people there does God want to fix?

_____

_____

Is there a place in your life in which you have been putting God off? What do you think God may be trying to teach or show you by continuing to speak to you about serving him?

_____

_____

_____

A Redemptive Purchase

The LORD said to me, "Go, show your love to your wife again, though she is loved by another and is an adulteress. Love her as the LORD loves the Israelites, though they turn to other gods and love the sacred raisin cakes." So I bought her for fifteen shekels of silver and about a homer and a lethek of barley. Then I told her, "You are to live with me many days; you must not be a prostitute or be intimate with any man, and I will live with you."

Hosea 3:1–3 NIV

The Big Picture

If anyone could claim to have a difficult marriage relationship, it would be the prophet from the Old Testament, Hosea. His wife, Gomer, did not share much in common with him. Hosea was consumed with living a life that honored God; Gomer was a known adulteress. He was intent on communicating a stern message that God would judge Israel for its own spiritual waywardness. Meanwhile, Gomer was given to marital unfaithfulness, serving as a living example of the harm that infidelity brings to a spiritual union. Because Hosea was a prophet of God, the fact that he married a known harlot was not overlooked by Israel, the nation to whom he prophesied. By marrying Gomer, he indicted Israel—a nation of descendants of slaves who repeatedly worshiped the golden calves of Egypt and other false gods—for also being a harlot.

Hosea and Gomer parented three children together. Just as Hosea's marriage to Gomer was a picture for all Israel of the spiritual union between God himself and the nation, so, too, did the naming of each child represent a larger, more significant spiritual reality speaking to the particular struggles that Israel would face for being unfaithful to God. Each of Hosea and Gomer's children also served as a representative picture of God's impending judgment upon the nation they called home.

Eventually, even the responsibilities of motherhood could not keep Gomer at home. Though married and united to Hosea, Gomer sold herself to another in the name of prostitution. She was completely enslaved by her lusts, and she chose her passion for lust over the security of a faithful husband, the joy of being a mother, and the peace of a stable family. Many scholars have concluded that Hosea and Gomer likely divorced because of her conduct and its effect on the family, which alludes to the broken relationship between God who is faithful and Israel, which was not.

Through it all, Hosea loved Gomer. At God's leading, Hosea sought out his wife. God had informed the prophet that he would find her in bondage to another, and that to claim her again as his bride, he would have to pay a ransom for her. So that is exactly what Hosea determined to do. He found her and paid the ransom to redeem her from the possession of another, even though their marriage vows had already bonded them to each other legally and spiritually. Hosea showed that love is about relationship, not about legal obligation, and that love always offers another chance.

You took my side, Master; you brought me back alive!

Lamentations 3:58 MSG

Take a
Closer Look

In this familiar story of Hosea's redemptive love toward his adulterous wife, Gomer, take the time to draw out the emphasis that God was willing to pay an expensive fee to redeem the people he already owned so that they could be restored back into relationship with him. The real-life example of Hosea shows that he paid fifteen shekels of silver and a measure of barley to buy back his wife. He did this so his wife would know he loved her. He did this so his wife could experience the freedom from being a slave to her lusts. He did this so they could know each other as husband and wife and not master and servant. At his time of purchase, he declared that he loved her, that she was restored to her full status, and that they would live together in the right relationship.

Several hundred years later, Jesus played the part of Hosea, and this time the entire world was Gomer, his unfaithful wife. However, this time fifteen shekels of silver and a measure of barley was not enough. To buy back his bride, he paid the expense with his own life. He did this freely so that the people of the world could be restored to a right relationship with him. By rights, everyone already belonged to him because he is God. Driven by love, he went the distance so everyone could know him intimately, rather than by a legal contract.

> The gospel comprises indeed, and unfolds, the whole mystery of man's redemption, as far forth as it is necessary to be known for our salvation.
>
> Robert Boyle

280   take a CLOSER look

Virtually everyone makes choices in life that they later regret because of the wedge those choices force between them and God. Whether the choice was a foolish one-time decision, or a willful stubbornness to disappoint God on an ongoing basis, every person at one time or another finds himself or herself distanced from God

because of sin. The good news is that God loves you enough to pay whatever expense to redeem you from the slums of life so you may be restored.

On the first, most important level, God already paid the price of his own Son, Jesus, so that you can be reunited with him. He gave this ransom so that you could know God personally and intimately. God never intended to have a distant, impersonal relationship with you. However, your unfaithfulness kept you separated until he paid the price to purchase you. Now you can be close again and speak with him as a wife would with her loving husband.

Just like Gomer, you may already have been identified as being united with God, but find yourself being tempted to go back to the life you used to know. The temptations are strong and alluring. Remember that those ways end in bondage, and God has remained faithful to you, so you could live in the joy, peace, and security of being close to him.

I know my living Redeemer, and He will stand on the dust at last.

Job 19:25 HCSB

How Others See It

The theme of spiritual purity that dominated the book of Hosea has reverberated throughout biblical history. In *Paul, Scripture and Ethics: A Study of 1 Corinthians 5–7*, Brian S. Rosner wrote:

"Just as Paul exhorted the Corinthians not to go to prostitutes, so in Hosea 3:3 Hosea commanded Gomer not to be a prostitute. Both admonitions of sexual purity are argued on similar grounds. Hosea's demand is based upon his special relationship with Gomer; he is her husband. . . . Calling God's people to repentance on the basis that he is their husband and master, far from divorcing Paul from his Scriptural heritage, places him in line with the best of Israel's prophets."

Tim LaHaye, Jerry B. Jenkins, and Frank Martin collaborate the position that Hosea's story is just as relevant today, in their book *Embracing Eternity*:

"It is our story put in the perspective of God. God redeemed us in spite of our contempt and rebellion, but the price God paid was far greater. In fact, it was unthinkable. He paid with the blood of his own son. Is it possible to comprehend the unconditional love of God? Probably not."

Zooming In

Hosea's name means "deliverer" and stems from a root term meaning "free, wide-open spaces." As with many of the prophets who would both precede and succeed him, his name hinted at the hope God offered to Israel. Just as Gomer was enslaved by her lusts, so, too, was Israel enslaved by its spiritual prostitution. God used Hosea as a living illustration that he offered Israel an opportunity to be delivered from its self-purchased shackles of sorrow, and that, by trusting God, the nation could experience the joy of freedom without constraint.

Gomer's name, on the other hand, also provides insight to Israel's plight. Her name means "completion." Her name, understood in the context of her life's failure, demonstrates the total futility of her situation. Just as Homer's bride found herself overwhelmed by moral failure, Israel's independence had resulted in a similar plight.

God has no partiality with the favor that he shows people. He offers to buy back or redeem every person who is struggling with something or someone who controls them, so that they will know his love.

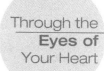

How do you identify with Gomer? What are the issues controlling you? How does it limit the joy you would like to experience in life?

Perhaps you have already received the love of God and call yourself a Christian. Have you ever had experiences like Gomer's where you fell back into old ways and destructive patterns? Do you desire to be free from those shackles by again trusting God over this for once and all?

The purchase of Gomer gave her the right standing to leave her old life behind. How would your life be different if you left behind your old life? What could you see improving because of it?

A Clear Choice

Fear the LORD, serve Him in sincerity and in truth, and put away the gods which your fathers served on the other side of the River and in Egypt. Serve the LORD! And if it seems evil to you to serve the LORD, choose for yourselves this day whom you will serve, whether the gods which your fathers served that were on the other side of the River, or the gods of the Amorites, in whose land you dwell. But as for me and my house, we will serve the LORD.

Joshua 24:14–15 NKJV

The Big Picture

Joshua was the fearless leader of Israel who received authority from God to take the nation out of four decades of wandering and settle them in the land that had been promised to them. Joshua had watched his nation's people for years, first as a scout for Moses, and now as their leader. In these people, he had seen a troubling trend of times of spiritual faithfulness followed by spiritual infidelity. Every time the situation grew dire, the people cried out against God and inclined themselves to abandoning God in the name of a foreign deity.

Joshua, though, had remained faithful. He had stayed committed to following God because he had seen God provide for his nation time and again. He remained loyal to God because he had seen God deliver his nation from adversary after adversary. Joshua had witnessed God overcome the mighty forces of Pharaoh, freeing the nation of Israel from the shackles of slavery.

He had protected Israel from Pharaoh's thundering chariots. God had driven out the Philistines, the Sidonians, the Geshurites, the Canaanites, the Avvites, the Amorites, the Gebalites, the Rephaites, the Hittites, the Perizzites, the Hivites, and the Jebusites, and others. God had overcome thirty-one different mighty provincial kings in giving the land over to the tribes of Israel.

Now Joshua was old and near the end of his life. He loved his nation and he loved God. He was fearful that the nation would again prove unfaithful in the face of a future threat or impending danger from a powerful foe. Joshua's opportunities to influence his followers would soon be ending, so he determined to spend his last breaths and final efforts reminding Israel of God's faithfulness in hope that the nation would choose likewise to remain faithful.

This passage records the final message Joshua spoke to the people of Israel, having assembled all the tribes together for a final gathering where the covenant between God and the nation would be renewed. He reminded the people of all that God had done through the years and of how God had honored his promises to Israel, and then he pressed the nation to make a choice, person by person and family by family. They could choose God, or they could choose something less. Joshua left no room for questions or ambiguity for his own choice; as their leader, and as the head of his household, they would be following God.

> *Blessings we enjoy daily, and for the most of them, because they be so common, men forget to pay their praises.*
>
> Izaak Walton

This passage records Joshua's famous declaration of his choice to follow God. However, give attention to the prior details to see that his choice was made on the heels of a negative alternative. His declaration that he and his household will serve the Lord is so forceful and courageous that it overwhelms and quickly overshadows the fact that a lesser alternative is available.

Israel still had to choose God. Even after all that God had done for them. After all the provision, after all the protection, after all the deliverance, after all the victories. At the end of Joshua's life, they still had to make a choice. The elderly leader understood the reality that choosing to be faithful to God required an ongoing choice because he had seen his nation choose wrongly too many times. He had witnessed their struggles as Israel wavered between disobedience and repentance.

In challenging the tribes of Israel and the families within those tribes to conscientiously choose God, Joshua underlined the reality that being faithful to God does not happen by accident or by coincidence. If the people of Israel were to be passive, then they certainly would soon be given to idolatry and wandering, just like their ancestors. Faithfulness requires proactive effort.

> *Never undertake anything for which you wouldn't have the courage to ask the blessings of heaven.*
>
> Georg Lichtenberg

People today need to see that following God requires an overt decision rather than a passive agreement. If you want your life to be known by a lack of spiritual integrity or by moral compromise, all you have to do is to do nothing. It will not be long before temptation finds you. It will not be long before you are distracted, deceived, or deluded.

It will not be long before you find yourself pulled in many different directions, none of which honor God.

If you look back in your life, you can see the fingerprints of God's faithfulness all through it. You can identify times where God carried you through a trauma. You can remember instances where God helped you overcome a challenge. You can recount experiences where God encouraged you, emboldened you, or exhorted you. You can relate to times where God examined you, redirected you, or refined you to succeed. God has been faithful, because that is who God is.

Choosing to serve God is nothing less than giving him all of your life in total surrender and obedience. It is trusting him in all details and counting on him to meet your needs. He has been faithful and promises to remain so. Today is your opportunity to do the same.

I do all this for the sake of the gospel, that I may share in its blessings.

1 Corinthians 9:23 NIV

Joshua's determination has long been applied to personal households throughout the generations. In retrospect, Joshua made the same determination for the household of Israel. In *Joshua: Mighty Warrior and Man of Faith,* W. Phillip Keller wrote:

"Not only had Joseph achieved amazing exploits for himself as a man, but he also brought all of his people to remarkable rest in the care of the Almighty. No leader ever started out with so little and ended with so much. Joshua had taken a shattered, woebegone, weary band of stragglers in the desert and forged them into a formidable Middle Eastern empire. He has seldom been given the full credit he deserves as possibly the greatest man of faith ever to set foot on the stage of human history."

Even with courageous spiritual leadership, people must still individually decide to honor God daily. W. Arden Clarke wrote in *An Analysis of Church Government*:

"As the children of Israel settled into their promised land, they made a decision—*their* decision! This reveals the *pattern,* the *character,* the *tone* of all of God's dealings with people throughout the history of the human race and God's relationship to them. . . . The *principle* is the same—*the people choose* whom they will serve and *they are accountable for their choices!*"

Zooming In

As Moses' apprentice, Joshua served as the Jewish leader's right-hand man. Originally, Joshua's name was Hoshea, which means "deliverer." Prior to delegating his helper to spy in the land of Canaan, Moses deliberately changed Hoshea's name to Joshua, which means "The Lord delivers." This subtle clarification would be an important reminder for the dangerous undertaking that would soon occur.

Joshua's father is mentioned several times in the Old Testament. His dad's name was Nun, and he was widely thought to have lived his entire life under the oppression of the Egyptian captivity, where most men were forced as slaves into the backbreaking, brickmaking work of building the massive pyramids.

Every day, you have many opportunities to choose God's way or your own way. Determine to follow Joshua's example. Choose God's option, no matter what others may do, and encourage others to do the same.

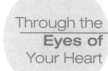

In what situations is it easy to choose God's way over your own way? Is it in areas such as going to church or living morally? Where is it more difficult? What about your entertainment choices or telling the truth? Why is it that some areas are more difficult than others?

What benefits can you see in choosing God's way in these difficult areas over the way you have been living in the past? What consequences have you had to pay for not choosing God's way previously?

It has been said that change is always more difficult until the pain of doing things the same way is more significant than the risk of doing things differently. God promises blessing for obedience. Do you see risks in choosing God's way? What are those risks? How are the potential benefits better than the risks?

A Command of Love

O Israel, you should listen and be careful to do it, that it may be well with you and that you may multiply greatly, just as the LORD, the God of your fathers, has promised you, in a land flowing with milk and honey. Hear, O Israel! The LORD is our God, the LORD is one! You shall love the LORD your God with all your heart and with all your soul and with all your might.

Deuteronomy 6:3–5 NASB

The Big Picture

All of Israel's twelve tribes surrounded Moses. The nation had been gathered to receive a word from their leader who had brought them out of bondage to the Egyptian pharaoh to the banks of the Jordan River. They could see the fulfillment of decades of promise across the shores of the wide, rushing river. On the other side of the mighty river lay the land that had been promised to them. They had seen God bless them when they had been obedient, and they had suffered through the difficulties of trying to make their way without God's leadership. The time had come for Moses to share the laws that God had given him to govern the people and establish a standard of living for the nation of Israel.

Moses began as he had before, in reiterating God's faithfulness in getting Israel to where they currently camped. He reminded them of their troubles, and of God's provision. He then repeated the Ten Commandments that God had imparted unto Moses as the standard for governing their civilization. With that, God bade Moses to send Israel to rest so God could spend more

take a CLOSER look

time with Moses, explaining all the rest of the laws that were designed to shape the nation.

From this extended time between Moses and God, the commandment Jesus declared to be the most important in the Bible came into being: "Love the LORD your God with all your heart and with all your soul and with all your might." This exhortation requires a total commitment to God, involving the intellectual, emotional, mental, logical, and even physical aspects of each individual. From the onset, God establishes a standard that declares that passive belief is insufficient, partial obedience is inadequate, and a passionless faith is ineffective.

God and Moses both understood the challenges that still lay ahead for this nation—the difficulties in establishing their claims of possession, the opposition from battle-ready enemies, the temptation to join in ungodly practices as their cultures intermingled and intermarried. God remembered Israel's past patterns of waywardness. In love, he commanded them to put him first rather than suffer the dire consequences of not doing so. By giving this command, he was equipping his nation with the greatest resource it needed for prosperity: himself.

A new commandment I give to you, that you love one another; as I have loved you, that you also love one another.

John 13:34 NKJV

Take a
Closer Look

A closer look at verse 3 shows that God commanded Israel to commit to a whole-person love effort so it would be well with them. Just as the command to love God was spiritual, physical, and material, so, too, is the promise he gives in return.

The opportunity to love God with the whole heart would give Israel a single passion for God. If they focused solely on God, they would not be swayed by false gods or enslaved by pagan rituals. They would not compromise themselves to marry people from opposing cultures who would constantly tempt them to betray their beliefs.

To love God with the entire soul meant that Israel would put their spiritual lives in the hands of God. They would trust him to fulfill his promises, to guide their paths, and to grant them favor.

To love God with all their strength meant that the people of Israel would put their feet behind their beliefs and go into battle believing that God went before them and that their victory was inevitable because God had already promised it to them.

Heart, soul, and strength—loving God completely commanded by a completely loving God. It was the promise of blessing.

Wherever the fear of God rules in the heart, it will appear both in works of charity and piety, and neither will excuse us from the other.

Matthew Henry

God commands you today to offer him a whole-person love. The reason he does this is the same for you as it was for the nation of Israel. He wants to bless you and prosper you.

Apply It
to Your Life

Such a love is not easy. It does not happen without an effort and a conscientious determination. To love God with all your heart means that you will constantly have to deny short-term affections that would compromise your love for God. Temptations that give instant gratification always carry a divine price tag. Loving God with all your soul means constantly giving your soul over to him—dying daily, so to speak—so that he can use you for the plans he has made. Loving God with all your strength means doing the one thing harder than dying for your faith: that is, living for it. God wants you to speak for truth, so that others will know it. He wants you to share his good news with others, and to share the news of the good work he is doing in you. God extends to you the same promise that he did your spiritual ancestors. Love him completely, and you will be glad you did.

Jesus answered: Love the Lord your God with all your heart, soul, and mind. This is the first and most important commandment. The second most important commandment is like this one. And it is, "Love others as much as you love yourself."

Matthew 22:37–39 CEV

Investing in God with all your heart, soul, and strength will pay spiritual dividends that will transform your life. Pat Morley wrote in *Devotions for the Man in the Mirror*:

"We are too busy. The suffocating pace of secular society subtly strangles our personal devotions. . . . Some of us have forgotten why we take time, and with whom we spend it. . . . Have you devoted yourself to looking for him with all your heart and all your soul? Or are your quiet times like a hot, dry breath from a desert wind? Go and meet with God. Do the first thing first. His breath is cool and refreshing. It is the Holy Spirit who will revive you."

Such an invitation is illustrative of the comprehensive relationship God desires to have with you. Lael Arrington describes it this way in *Godsight: Renewing the Eyes of Our Hearts*:

"The Greatest commandment is about intensity: 'Love the Lord your God with all your heart, soul, mind, and strength.' Again and again throughout scripture, he invites us to turn to him with all our hearts, trust him with all our hearts, serve him with all our hearts, obey him with all our hearts. . . . What God wants is intensity. . . . We are invited to seek God with an intensity that honors his desire for us."

Zooming **In**

The book of Deuteronomy is part of the Jewish *Tanakh*, or holy book, and consists of the laws given by God to Moses to govern the people of Israel. The book can be arranged into three segments. The first recounts the faithful history of God among his people. The second is the presentation of the laws to guide them, and the final is the promise of blessing upon those who obey and punishment for those who disobey.

Some scholars have questioned how Moses could have written all of the first five of the Old Testament books since his death and burial are detailed within them. This challenged some to reason that possibly Joshua ap-pended the book with these details. However, most religious leaders of ancient Judaism and Christianity agree with the numerous references in the Bible that establish Moses as the author, which suggests he wrote about his death and burial prophetically.

Loving God requires every aspect of who you are—emotionally, spiritually, and physically. Give God this whole-person type of love and experience the blessing of loving the same way you are loved.

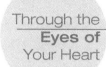

Through the
Eyes of
Your Heart

What does it mean to love with all your heart? What other things do you love "with all your heart"? Is it possible to love more than one thing in this way? Is it appropriate to do so?

Loving God with all your soul speaks to spiritual love. How is loving God with all your soul different from emotional "heart love"? If "heart love" is based upon emotions, what is "soul love" based upon? How is the spiritual aspect of love important to your holistic relationship with God?

Loving God completely requires physical effort. Why do you suppose it takes "all your strength" to love God? What forces and temptations have to be overcome physically to love God? What effect does this love have on the way you emotionally and spiritually love God?

Introductions

Israel, that is what I will do to you, and since I will do that to you, Israel, prepare to meet your God! He is here: the One who forms the mountains, creates the wind, and reveals His thoughts to man, the One who makes the dawn out of darkness and strides on the heights of the earth. Yahweh, the God of Hosts, is His name.

Amos 4:12–13 HCSB

The Big Picture

The nation of Israel claimed to be God's people, but they chose not to follow him. They intermingled with other cultures and allowed their own spiritual culture to become tainted by the introduction of false gods and idols into their own worship. All through this and surrounding lands, people acknowledged the reality of God, but consistently lived in a manner that dishonored him.

While this took place, an unknown sheepherder lived a life of purity and encountered God. The herder—a man of no repute or wealth—communed with God and communicated with him. God spoke to this man named Amos and told the shepherd to introduce him to Israel as their father and Lord. Amos did what a poor, godly sheepherder who was not distracted by wealth, success, or selfishness should do: he obeyed.

He immediately started sharing the message of God's judgment with the duplicitous but successful merchants of Israel. He eventually would decry the

take a CLOSER look

lack of justice and mercy that was rampant throughout the land, and would even be accused of trying to divide the country and undermine the leadership of the king. Amos never compromised God's message, calling the nation to social and personal repentance.

Amos was a simple man with a simple message. It was not sufficient for people who claimed to be the children of God to behave as though they were spiritually orphaned. It dishonored God for the people of Israel to behave in such a manner. He warned that unless they altered their course of conduct, they would find themselves exiled from their own country, a nation whose home would be occupied by unsympathetic invaders.

Amos appealed to his countrymen to turn back to the God they claimed to know and live like they said they believed. The nation of Israel was not a people who did not know the right conduct or way of thinking. They had simply abandoned God's ways in deference to their own whims and desires.

This straight-talking sheepherder spoke plainly that even in the specter of exile, God offered hope. God took the initiative to speak through Amos, so that Israel could avoid the impending judgment. Unfortunately, they more often than not responded as though God were not Lord, but a stranger to be feared and kept at a distance.

God is unchanging in His love. He loves you. He has a plan for your life. Do not let the newspaper headlines frighten you. God is still sovereign; he's still on the throne.

Billy Graham

Amos is a book known for its prophecy of judgment against wayward humanity. In this passage, a closer look reveals that God took the first step in speaking to Israel by reintroducing himself to them. Through this encouraging self-introduction, God showed his power over creation and that he is available to make his will known to man. God showed his ability to guide people in his ways and his interest in doing so.

Amos dealt with successful people who were filled with a sense of accomplishment. Their industries flourished while their morality fell bankrupt. In refamiliarizing Israel with the God for whom Amos spoke, he introduced them to the one who created the mighty mountains, who raises and sets the day's sun, and who established the stars in the sky. For a hard-to-impress community, the sense of perspective that Amos provided was humbling and appropriate. Amos reoriented the people around him to consider their own accomplishments in light of God's much greater, more significant accomplishments. In doing so, he was illustrating that because they never knew they would encounter an adversary who was even greater than they were, they could find solace and comfort in trusting the God who is bigger and more accomplished than everyone else.

> *I have lived a long time, sir, and the longer I live the more convincing proofs I see of this truth—that God governs in the affairs of men.*
>
> Benjamin Franklin

Even if your own life is incredibly successful and marked by victory upon success, you never know what difficulties wait in your future. Today's good fortune could give way to tomorrow's misfortune. In times of success, the temptation that many people face is to forget about God as the one who provided them with the blessings they enjoy.

Apply It to Your Life

This passage shows that God is not only the incredible Creator of all things, but he is also the one who reveals his thoughts to people. This shows that God intentionally creates for the benefit of humanity, so that men and women might understand how they fit within the vastness of the world, and how their successes and failures play a part in God's bigger picture.

When you run into a problem, you may feel as if that situation is a steep mountain to climb, or that the wind is in your face, or even that you are in the dark. For each of these comparisons, Amos offers you the biblical encouragement that God is the one who formed the mountains, who guides the wind, and who brings dawn to the dark. As God reveals his plans for you, he wants you to remember him as the one who is bigger than your obstacles, and he is available to help you overcome.

Let the heavens be glad and the earth rejoice, and let them say among the nations, "The Lord is King!"

1 Chronicles 16:31 HCSB

Just like Israel in the time of Amos, people today can become so familiar with prosperity, blessing, and success that they forget God is the giver of these benefits. In *Walking Through the Bible with HMS Richards*, the author writes:

"The existence of God is proved by the existence of the universe. Every effect must have an adequate cause. There is design in the world, so there must have been a designer. . . . All things must have had an origin, a beginning, a creation. Creation by chance is absurd, for to say that a thing is caused with no cause for its production, is to say that a thing is effected when it is effected by nothing. All things, then, that do appear, must have been created by some being. That being is God."

R. Kent Hughes, in *Disciplines of a Godly Man*, posits that this Amos-oriented view of God is appropriate for proper worship:

"It is important that we understand, in distinction of the popular view that worship is for us, that worship begins not with man as its focus, but God. Worship must be orchestrated and conducted with the vision before us of an august, awesome, holy transcendent who is to be pleased and, above all, glorified by our worship."

Zooming **In**

Amos served as a prophet in the times of the kingdoms of Jeroboam (son of Joash) in Israel, and Uzziah in Judah. Amos was not a "professional prophet" in the sense that he did not serve in the court of either king. Rather, he was simply a sheepherder and a fig farmer. He came in from outside the established religious system to remind God's people from where their blessings originated.

A common refrain from Amos was his declaration that "the day of the Lord" would soon arrive. People who had believed in the God of Israel had long looked forward to this event as a time of victory and celebration. However, Amos warned them because of their independent spirit that had separated them from relying upon God, this soon-coming day would be marked by sorrow and judgment.

The God who formed the universe with his spoken command and who named each star wants you to know him personally and intimately so you can rely upon him in times of need. Familiarize yourself with him today and rely upon him for the challenges you will meet tomorrow.

Where do you see the power and might of God in creation? What aspect of creation is most impressive to you—majestic mountains, raging rivers, or furious winds? How can these physical realities help shape a respect-filled view of God?

Where do you see the unique problem-solving creativity of God? What aspects of this demonstration of God's ingenuity impress you most—the diversity of the human cell, the elaborate effectiveness of the water cycle, or the fine balance of the solar system? How can these physical realities help you trust God with your seemingly unsolvable problems?

Where do you see the positive effects of God's solutions? Which outcomes of God's provision impact you most—is it in a loving family, a faithful friend, or an encouraging church? How can the physical realities of God's provision encourage you the next time you feel lonely, or even alone with a problem?

Taking Peace for Granted

Since we have been declared righteous by faith, we have peace with God through our Lord Jesus Christ. Also through Him, we have obtained access by faith into this grace in which we stand, and we rejoice in the hope of the glory of God.

Romans 5:1–2 HCSB

The Big Picture

The multicultural Roman population thrived in an atmosphere where social standing was vital. Every citizen knew where he stood in relation to his neighbors, colleagues, and competitors. In a stringent, structured system that kept detailed records about an individual's and family's class and status based on heritage, ancestry, and profession, societal rank was the undercurrent that hindered or empowered each person through life. Romans implored the gods to give them a good reputation in their trade and to grant them success in their endeavors based on their good standing as being fair, trustworthy, and honorable. To become known as dishonest, scheming, or unethical was to invite scorn from the deities and exclusion from the community of peers.

At the same time, the Jewish community was equally concerned with their standing and reputation among peers and within the larger context of the Roman community. They desired to be separate and distinct from the Romans with whom they shared the city, and they were equally proud of their spiritual fidelity and religious identity.

This elevated emphasis in spirituality existed ironically in a society that was known for immoral indulgences, carnal excesses, and continual violation of the laws of God and men. Accordingly, the majority of the population—regardless of their cultural practice—found themselves wavering between the extremes of piety and wickedness.

Paul understood this tension that existed among the Roman citizens, and he offered them a message of hope in the gospel of Jesus. His message was revolutionary because it redefined how a person could both approach and relate to God. Paul told all of Rome that if they would place their faith in Jesus as God's Messiah, they could once and forever be found righteous. No longer would their right standing among God and men be dependent upon a ritual, a sacrifice, or time spent in a pagan temple or a Jewish synagogue. They would be perpetually in good standing with God and because of that, would be at peace with him.

Peace with God was a message that resonated among the people of Rome, who had long known of war and conquest. Eager for peace and desiring righteousness, Jew and Gentile alike responded to the good news Paul shared, and the peace of Christianity advanced in a land that before was rife with war and conflict.

If we have not quiet in our minds, our outward comfort will do no more for us than a golden slipper on a gouty foot.

John Bunyan

Today people are just as concerned about having a good standing (righteousness) with God and with other people. The initial verses of Romans 5 focus on God's offer of declared righteousness and peace that allow a person to persevere through the difficulties of life. A closer look shows that God offers more than righteousness or good standing. He extends an olive branch of peace through the conduit of faith. By faith, a person can experience the calm reality of grace in a world sorely lacking it.

In a Roman society known by conquest, violence, and social turbulence, the peacemakers known as Christians were quiet revolutionaries. They met in small groups and rather than indulging in extravagancies for which they would later have to apologize at their gods' altars, they would pray together, explore God's Scriptures together, and share God's message of grace over and again with anyone who would hear it. They walked and talked with the calm confidence of a people who understood the mysteries of eternity, who knew the God Romans had previously thought to be unknowable, and let that personal knowledge of God shape their lives in word, thought, and deed.

> *A great many people are trying to make peace, but that has already been done. God has not left it for us to do; all we have to do is enter into it.*
>
> Dwight L. Moody

Only when you know you are at peace with your Creator can you truly face the trials of life with eternal confidence and assurance. If you have confidence in standing in front of God because he has unconditionally approved of you through your faith in Jesus, then standing before your fellow man is immensely less intimidating.

God offers just that opportunity, and this Scripture reveals that such an offer is nothing less than undeserved grace. God's standard is so impossibly high that it can never be met through effort or religious act. By his own goodwill, God extends grace to you so that you can have peace with him that would be otherwise unattainable. Consequently, having peace with God allows you to thrive in a world where peace is a rare commodity.

All around you, peace is either illusory or a tenuous apprehension, liable to break at the first cross word or differing opinion. Through your peace-filled relationship with God, you can be like your spiritual ancestors and be a peaceful revolutionary to this warring, conflicted world. You will have the ability to persevere through your own times of difficulty, and you will help others do the same by extending an encouraging word of truth about God's love that is available to them as well.

You will keep in perfect peace him whose mind is steadfast, because he trusts in you. . . . LORD, you establish peace for us; all that we have accomplished you have done for us.

Isaiah 26:3, 12 NIV

Peace with God allows for effectiveness in your external relationships with other people. Even so, as Watchman Nee details in *The Normal Christian Life*, it occurs while still at conflict internally with yourself:

"Now that I have forgiveness of sins, God will no longer be a cause of dread to me. . . . I very soon find, however, that I am going to be a great cause of trouble to myself. There is still unrest within, for within me there is still something that draws me to sin. There is peace with God, but there is no peace with myself. There is in fact civil war in my own heart."

Ruth Paxon, in *Life on the Highest Plane,* explained that peace is found internally when you understand how God brought peace to you in Jesus:

"Certain definite and glorious blessings are secured to the believer. Chief among these is peace with God. . . . All distance between God and the sinner is obliterated. All barriers are torn down. The believer is made near God's heart through the blood of Jesus. . . . The reconciliation was effected through the self-provided, suffering reconciliation through God in Christ."

Zooming **In**

The concept of reconciliation is more than just two sides coming to terms with one another, as it may be understood today. The biblical word picture is that where one side is radically changed into compliance with the other, often at the expense of extreme opposition. To be reconciled to God means to have all that is in you opposing him to be set aside so that you are compliant to him.

The first thing that Jesus said to the disciples was "peace!" This declaration was both encouraging and revolutionary, in that every expectation from the followers' perspective was that they were a part of a countercultural group that would overcome the Roman and Jewish establishment by conflict, under the victorious leadership of their Messiah. Jesus established a new paradigm in sending out his followers with a message of peace and reconciliation.

Living peacefully with others is a direct effect of having peace with God. Make the effort to have your personal relationships match the nature of your spiritual relationships and experience peace in daily living.

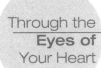

Through the
Eyes of
Your Heart

The Bible says that Jesus grew in favor with both God and man. If Jesus was able to grow in this way, so can you. Where do you see that you have growth potential with God? With others?

Remember that God's grace—his unmerited love and kindness for you—covers all of your life. What does it mean to you to "stand in grace"? What are some areas in your life where you may tend to give less grace or be more judgmental? Why is it difficult to extend grace in these areas of your life? What biblical truths help you apply grace to others more readily?

The basis of your right standing with God is based upon the peace-bringing effort of Jesus, not on something you did. How can you live in peace with someone who is not doing anything to live peacefully with you? What do you have to give up to embrace peace with others?

God's Two Sents

> *The same day at evening, being the first day of the week, when the doors were shut where the disciples were assembled, for fear of the Jews, Jesus came and stood in the midst, and said to them, "Peace be with you." When He had said this, He showed them His hands and His side. Then the disciples were glad when they saw the Lord. So Jesus said to them again, "Peace to you! As the Father has sent Me, I also send you."*
>
> John 20:19–21 NKJV

The Big Picture

The followers of Jesus were in hiding. They were fearful for their very lives. They believed they had aligned themselves with the most important political and social leader of world history, thinking they were on the cusp of overthrowing oppressive Roman overlords and being free from the religious strictures of the Pharisees. They had marched into Jerusalem at the time of the feast with victory parades and celebrations on their minds, already organizing plans for their own place in the political cabinet of Jesus' new administration.

Now, three days later, all their plans were in shambles. Reduced to a huddled group of cowering refugees, the followers of Jesus mourned his death and worried about what to do next. Any hopes of a revolution had been crushed when the Romans and Pharisees executed Jesus. Earlier this morning, they had heard the report that Jesus was missing from the tomb, that the stone protecting it had rolled away, and that Mary herself had an encounter with Jesus, who had risen from the dead.

Emotions were on edge, reason seemed impossible, and staying hidden seemed the safest course of action. Suddenly, Jesus appeared in their midst. Scarcely could anything be more terrifying than the unexpected instant appearance in a locked, secluded room of the Lord they had seen murdered and had personally buried. Now he stood among them, available to be touched. Jesus was alive!

Not only was he there in physical form, but he spoke to them. His first words articulated a message of peace and hope. True to his nature, he brought calm to his followers, tempering their fears with his reassuring presence and soothing words. He evidenced his control over all their worries, able to overcome the greatest obstacle—death itself—to be among them and to once again lead them.

The group eventually calmed and even became glad that Jesus was in their midst. There is no way to know which followers immediately returned to thoughts of military overthrow and conquest. Regardless of the thoughts and opinions that may have existed that night at Jesus' return, the Messiah quickly set the agenda for the mission in store for his disciples.

The revolution would take place. They would soon open their doors and strike out against the world. As Jesus invited them into service, their understanding of the scope of the war would radically expand, as well as their understanding of how to engage the enemy.

Where our deep gladness and the world's deep hunger meet, we hear a further call.

Frederick Buechner

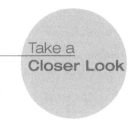

This faithful passage has served as the foundation behind centuries of goodwill offerings between believers. Look closer and see that Jesus not only brought peace to frightened followers through his work on the cross (as evidenced by his wounds), but today he sends believers into a frightened world with the same message of hope and healing.

Jesus did not concern himself with the tyranny of the Romans, or of the constricting, murderous plotting of the Pharisees. Jesus had his own agenda, and it began when he willingly left heaven on his own volition and came to earth in human form. Now, just as he had been sent by his Father in heaven, Jesus now sent out his own followers.

Jesus knew they would meet opposition; he had already warned them about what they would encounter. Yet, just as Jesus had extended mercy, delivered grace, performed miracles, and shared the news of the coming kingdom of God, he directed his disciples to do the same.

The end of their time together was soon approaching. He would spend just a little more time with them, and then they would be sent out to reproduce what they had witnessed him produce over the previous three years. They would go as Jesus had gone, and succeed as Jesus had.

> *Everyone has his own specific vocation or mission in life; everyone must carry out a concrete assignment that demands fulfillment. Therein he cannot be replaced, nor can his life be repeated, thus, everyone's task is unique as his specific opportunity to implement it.*
>
> Viktor Frankl

If you are a Christian, you have a purpose. God spoke authoritatively on numerous matters through his Son, Jesus. One of the final messages God communicated through him was that all those who would follow Jesus would therefore be sent out into the world to do the same work and accomplish the same feats as Jesus himself.

Apply It
to Your Life

You may not heal a leper or confront a demoniac in your lifetime. You may not debate a religious opponent or protect an adulterous woman from being murdered by religious zealots. However, God has sent you into this world just as he sent his own Son.

Why has God sent you out into the world? He is driven by an all-consuming love for his children. Having already claimed you for heaven through Jesus, God now employs you to share truth with others for the same cause, so that more people will know Jesus as Lord and have a relationship with God. This does not mean that you need to be a great communicator or a convincing persuader. You simply need to be genuine and willing to tell the story of what God did for you through Jesus.

Truly, anyone who welcomes my messenger is welcoming me, and anyone who welcomes me is welcoming the Father who sent me.

John 13:20 NLT

Being sent by God, Jesus came with a mission and purpose. Likewise, followers of Jesus are intentionally commissioned. In *Intercessory Prayer: How God Can Use Your Prayers to Move Heaven and Earth*, Dutch Sheets wrote:

"A representative is a 'sent' one. Sent ones have authority, as long as they represent the sender. And the importance or emphasis is not upon the sent one but the sender. The setting of conditions or the ability to carry out or enforce them is all the responsibility of the sender, not the sent one. . . . Jesus was a sent one. That is why he had authority. He received it from the father who sent him. . . . In essence, he was not really doing the works, but the father who sent him. . . . The same is true with us. Our authority comes from being sent ones, representing Jesus. As long as we function in that capacity, we function in Christ's authority. And in essence, we are not really doing the works, he is."

Zooming **In**

The Upper Room where Jesus brought peace and hope to the frightened disciples was the scene of several significant spiritual events. It was additionally where the Last Supper took place, where Jesus washed the apostles' feet, and where the Holy Spirit would later anoint Christ's followers for their mission to spread the gospel throughout the world.

The Greek word for *sent* is *apostelo*, which is the root for the word *apostle*. The word literally means "sent forth." Jesus told his followers that as God had sent him forth for the important work that he was about to complete, so, too, are Christ's followers sent forth to accomplish work designed by God specifically for them.

God sent Jesus to you. Jesus now sends you to others. Whether with a kind word or a good deed, you can bring hope to others, packaged with peace.

Through the
Eyes of
Your Heart

Who are some people you know who seem to struggle with being at odds with others? How can you bring them peace?

_____

_____

_____

_____

Think of people you know who need hope. What has caused them to lose hope? What are practical things you can do to encourage them?

_____

_____

_____

_____

What does it mean to you to be sent into the world? Where would you like to go "into the world" and what would you like to do? What will it take to do it?

_____

_____

_____

_____

Author Unknown

Time is God's way of keeping every-thing from happening at once.

We know that God causes all things to work together for good to those who love God, to those who are called according to His purpose.

Romans 8:28 NASB

J. Elder Cumming

In almost every case the beginning of new blessing is a new revelation of the character of God—more beautiful, more wonderful, more precious.

*If anyone is in Christ, there is a new
creation; old things have passed away,
and look, new things have come.*

2 Corinthians 5:17 HCSB

Benjamin Franklin

The Constitution only guarantees the American people the right to pursue happiness. You have to catch it yourself.

*Always be joyful. Keep on praying.
No matter what happens, always be
thankful, for this is God's will for you
who belong to Christ Jesus.*

1 Thessalonians 5:16–18 NLT

Your responsibility is to
hold your peace 9

Your perception of Jesus
correlates to your PURSUIT
of Jesus.